Landor's Poetry

Landor's Poetry

ROBERT PINSKY

The University of Chicago Press
Chicago & London

Library of Congress Catalog Card Number: 68-26760

The University of Chicago Press, Chicago 60637
The University of Chicago Press, Ltd., London W.C. 1
Published 1968. Printed in the United States of America

To Ellen and to Jim

Acknowledgments

The following people have read all or part of this book in manuscript, and have made it better by offering their valuable criticism and encouragement (none of them, however, should be associated with my mistakes or my opinions): David Bady, Charles Fifer, Hugh Kenner, Robert Maniquis, James McMichael, Peter Najarian, Ellen Pinsky, Robert Polhemus, William Sheidley, Wilfred Stone, and David Thorburn.

To Albert J. Guerard I have a special debt. His generosity and guidance have been too varied to summarize; among other things, he first suggested to me that I (or someone) ought to write about Landor's poetry.

Contents

ix

Landor
and Two Modern Poet-Critics

What made the ceiling waterproof?
Landor's tarpaulin on the roof.

W. B. Yeats, "A Nativity"

This book explores Landor's repeated use of subjects which came to him from tradition, or which he made to appear traditional. I associate this procedure with the very old rhetorical tradition of places and common-places, and I try to show that in harking back to such a tradition Landor was unique among Romantic poets. A "commonplace," in the relevant definition, is a stock truth legitimately used for the purposes of composition.

At the very least the concept of the commonplace provides, with similar distinctions, a means of clarifying the distracting and sometimes tiresome debate about the exact nature of Landor's reputed Classicism.[1] If Landor's work does reflect the pecu-

1. This appears to be the persistent center of attention in Landor studies. In R. H. Super's article "Walter Savage Landor," pp. 252–55 in Lawrence H. Houtchens' *The English Romantic Poets and Essayists: A Review of Research and Criticism* (New York: Modern Language Association of America, 1957), the summary alone includes: F. E. Pierce, "The Hellenic Current in English Nineteenth Century Poetry" (1917); R. I. Goldmark, *Studies in the Influence of the Classics on English Literature* (1918); E. Nitchie, "The Clas-

liar conception of "subject" which I think it does, then his excellence would have to be that of an innovator in matters of form — not an innovator who breaks or abandons traditional forms, but one who exploits, combines, and furthers them.

This role is very like the one attributed to Landor by Ezra Pound. A great believer in the history of form as a valid sort of history, Pound assigns to Landor a perhaps preposterous degree of importance as a contributor to the development of English poetic style. This high estimate appears to rest upon an idea resembling that proposed in the following pages: in an age of poetic "metaphysics" and new kinds of subject, Landor was concerned with style as a value in itself; thus, he was led to a kind of endeavor, often successful, which was unique among his contemporaries. This idea has the virtue of being fairly obvious, and gains further recommendation from its use by a younger poet-critic, Donald Davie, who is as different from Pound in his estimation of Landor as he is in other ways.

Davie uses the word "commonplace" several times in a short but valuable chapter on Landor.[2] Such corroboration of the usefulness of this concept, if not of one's admiration for Landor, is significant, for Davie seems to me worthy of serving with Pound among the small number of modern critics, mostly poets, who offer judgments, beyond mere "readings," of poems. Landor's oddly vital significance in the history of English verse is clarified if we compare the reasons with which Pound and Davie color — quite differently — the same version of the facts. Coming at different moments, and with different projects as poets, both men fulfill Pound's definition of the worthiest literary criticism:

---

sicism of Walter Savage Landor" (1919); E. Nitchie, *Virgil and the English Poets* (1919); Douglas Bush, *Mythology and the Romantic Tradition in English Poetry* (1937); S. A. Larrabee, *English Bards and Grecian Marbles* (1943); S. B. Beach, "Hellenism and the Modern Spirit" (1946); A. Gossman, "Landor and the 'Higher Fountains'" (1955); E. de Selincourt, "Classicism and Romanticism in the Poetry of Walter Savage Landor" (1930–31, 1932).

2. Donald Davie, "Landor's Shorter Poems," *Purity of Diction in English Verse* (London: Chatto and Windus, 1952), pp. 183–96.

> The value of criticism in proportion to actual making, is less
> than one to one hundred. The only critical formulations that
> rise above this level are the specifications made by artists who
> later put them into practice and achieve demonstrations.[3]

But the corollary danger of the poet-critic is that he has, inevitably, a bias or program which will, perhaps covertly, pervade even his critical treatment of quite particular matters.
And in relation to Landor, who seems to "mean" something to
poets, the critic's program is likely to be especially pervasive,
even if no more obvious. Yeats in "To A Young Beauty" ("And
I may dine at journey's end / With Landor and with Donne") is
not the only poet to use Landor's name nearly as a word:

> *Peace! there is peace at last.*
> *Deep in the Tuscan shade,*
> *Swathed in the Grecian past,*
> *Old Landor's bones are laid.*
> ....
>
> *Come, write good verses, then!* [4]

And so, the aspect of Landor's work which I think most interests the moderns Pound and Davie is contained in a tired yet
true observation about Landor: he has always been a poet's
poet. Wordsworth, Southey, Shelley, Swinburne, Browning,
Hopkins, Frost, Pound, Yeats — nearly everybody has visited
the slightly out-of-the-way shrine. They are drawn to Landor,
we can guess, because he is the poet of a way of writing; his uni-
fying concern is not an attitude toward love, theology, "nature,"
human folly, or a "system" — rather, the distinguishing intensity in Landor's work is supplied by an attitude toward language, toward the making, stylistic powers of the mind.

Indeed, as I suggest in my third chapter, this preoccupation is
often an explicit subject, in "Ye Who Have Toiled" and in
many other poems about writing. But perhaps even more im-

3. Ezra Pound, *Pavannes and Divagations* (London: Peter Owen, Ltd.,
1960), p. 96.
4. Yvor Winters, "Anacreontic," *Selected Poems* (Denver: Swallow Publi-
cations, 1960), p. 72.

portantly it is implicit in poems not merely about writing. Landor not only wrote well, but he also had a peculiar, extreme concern for the idea of writing well, and this concern modified every subject he touched. The emotional significance of this preoccupation is less immediately manifest than is a kind of "imagery," or a consistent kind of diction (erotic, technical, religious, regional), and the suavely deliberate concerns of Landor's verse have by tradition appeared in their full seriousness mostly to poets. To them he often embodies, apparently, a particular problem in poetic values, as is illustrated in the treatment of Landor — the poet of "writing well" — by Pound and Davie.

One must consider the originality which Pound claims for Landor's style by examining the form of Landor's blank verse, and, by concentrating on the diction in some of the shorter poems, one can judge the failure which Davie finds in Landor's use of the rhetorical commonplace. In any case, Pound is Landor's most eminent advocate, and Davie's chapter is to my knowledge the best essay on Landor's poems. I think that attention to the relation between Landor and each of these modern poets can suggest Landor's value and significance for modern readers of poetry. If I am right, this significance should emerge in the course of my argument, but I should like to offer a brief summary of Landor's significance, as I see its outlines, in relation to Pound and to Davie.

Ezra Pound

Both men view Landor as an experimenter. Pound comes at the font of a revolution, sure (at least in relation to the previous establishment) of "how to write," priest and publicist of a new "hardness" of style in English verse.

In a chronological list of twenty-five authors "through whom the metamorphosis of English verse-writing may be traced,"

Pound mentions only Landor between Crabbe and Browning.[5] In a "recapitulation," he places Landor in an extraordinary tripartite progression which begins with Chaucer and Shakespeare, speaking of Landor as "so far ahead of his English times that the country couldn't contain him." [6] And even beyond this enormous importance to more or less immediately subsequent writers, Landor was "driving piles into the mud, and preparing foundations — which have been largely unused by his successors." [7]

Outrageous estimate indeed! And, yes, outrageous even if one points out that *Gebir* had a powerful underground reputation among poets years before Coleridge, Scott, De Quincey, Southey, or Wordsworth even knew the author's name; that *Gebir* was an eighteenth-century poem, written before 1798; and that the clean, sweet blank verse of that quirky narrative may have been the first since the Commonwealth to avoid the awful twin lodestones of pentameter: what Pound calls "the Miltonian quagmire" and, on the other side, the pseudo-Popian slide rule.

> one morning he [Hogg] burst into Shelley's rooms at University College to tell him something of importance but found him so engrossed in *Gebir* that he would attend to nothing else, whereupon Hogg snatched the book out of his hand and flung it out the window — but a servant who was passing brought it in again, and Shelley was once more caught in its spell. There was something in the poem that caught his fancy, and he would read it aloud to others, or to himself, with a tiresome pertinacity.[8]

We know further, to extend the argument by authority, that De Quincey, Lamb, and Southey were, in less Shelleyan ways, also fascinated by the obscure and anonymous little book.

This contemporary attention was deserved. Had Landor died at twenty-two, one could still begin a partial defense of Pound's rather Orphic praise simply by comparing the blank verse of

5. Ezra Pound, *ABC of Reading* (New York: New Directions, 1960), p. 173.
6. *Ibid.*, p. 187.
7. *Ibid.*
8. R. H. Super, *Walter Savage Landor: A Biography* (New York: New York University Press, 1954), p. 69.

Gebir, for variety of subject, tone, and movement, with all pre-ceding post-Miltonic blank verse. The story is extravagant and the subject is miscellaneous, but the plot moves gracefully enough with what must have been the equivalent of motion-picture speed for an audience familiar with other narratives of *Gebir*'s genre. The narrative form gave Landor opportunities to show Shelley *et al.* how many and various kinds of situation his style could handle. That flexibility, especially when treating small, sharp details of human behavior or physical nature, must constitute much of Landor's appeal to his contemporaries and to Pound.

The passages most often quoted from *Gebir* are the descriptive ones, of which there are many kinds. The famous seashell is one of the less original, but will serve as a first example:

> *But I have sinuous shells, of pearly hue*
> *Within, and they that lustre have imbibed*
> *In the sun's palace porch; where, when unyoked,*
> *His chariot wheel stands midway in the wave.*
> *Shake one, and it awakens, then apply*
> *Its polished lips to your attentive ear,*
> *And it remembers its august abodes,*
> *And murmurs as the ocean murmurs there.*
> *And I have others, given me by the nymphs,*
> *Of sweeter sound than any pipe you have.*
> *Book I, lines 170–79*

There are similar passages of "good description" in Thomson, but they are likely to be less efficient because Thomson's prac-tice is to compensate for the absence of rhyme by careful atten-tion to "nobility" — that is, by a sometimes frantic stream of Miltonisms. The result of this enforced "elevation" is a tend-ency toward overemphasis which, like a stiff backache, hinders Thomson from stooping to the smaller sort of snow scene, let alone the whorls of a sea shell. Furthermore, Thomson, al-though he could perhaps have written seven of the above lines, could not have embedded them in the modest, if stylized, con-versation which I represent by including the last two lines.

I think that these subdued conversational lines are more impressive, considered historically, than the descriptive set piece, which is itself admirably free from any awkward booming of the medium. The third and fourth lines are compressed with such deft clarity that one hardly notices that they are a refinement upon a whole school of elaborate metaphor. But it is the conversation which testifies that *Gebir* is more than just a very refined version of eighteenth-century blank verse. Landor's characters, though hardly human, approach humanity to an appealing degree, mythological but not Mythical. One more quotation from *Gebir*, although perhaps not conclusive proof of anything, should exemplify the tone I mean, which I associate with Pound's "hardness." The heroine Charoba realizes that she loves the foreign prince Gebir, but she cannot quite tell Dalica, her nurse:

> *And now Charoba was alone, her heart*
> *Grew lighter; she sat down, and she arose,*
> *She felt voluptuous tenderness, but felt*
> *That tenderness for Dalica; she prais'd*
> *Her kind attention, warm solicitude,*
> *Her wisdom — for what wisdom pleased like hers!*
> *She was delighted: would she not behold*
> *Gebir? she blush'd; but she had words to speak,*
> *She form'd them and reform'd them, with regret*
> *That there was somewhat lost with every change:*
> *She could replace them — what would that avail —*
> *Moved from their order they have lost their charm.*

The passage is not a high point, not a great scene, but it comes between such scenes; that it fulfills such a role with grace is worth noticing. Though the subject is meltingly soft and the sentences are fairly relaxed, nearly idiomatic, there is nevertheless a quality of hardness and rigor about the most prominent technique: namely, the careful use of the runover line as a sort of substitute for rhyme. The line-endings function very precisely in lending the lines that force which arises from the play of abstract form upon content; such is Landor's "hardness."

In Pound's essay "The Hard and Soft in French Poetry," "hardness" is exemplified by Gautier in French and Landor in English.

> Indeed, Gautier might well be the logical successor to Landor, were he not in all probability the logical co-heir with Landor of certain traditions.[9]

"Hardness" (which is always a virtue, while "softness" is sometimes a fault) is dependent, says Pound, neither upon originality of subject nor upon any great break with traditional verse forms. As it emerges in this essay, "hardness" is a project, very similar to the idea that poetic profundity may be achieved through primary attention to the details of emotion and technique; this devotion is the opposite of a commitment directly to the problems of finding a new poetic language and original subject. A few more quotations from Pound's criticism show his emphasis upon a writer's mastery of the numerous small decisions which have relatively little to do with originality of conception as we usually think of it:

> Histories of English literature always slide over translation — I suppose it is inferiority complex — yet some of the best books in English are translations [10]

Originality of conception as one usually thinks of it is a cliché: the true conception emerges in the course of stylistic labor. Thus Pound refers with admiration to "the tradition in Provence that it was considered plagiarism to take another man's form, just as it is now considered plagiarism to take his subject matter or plot." He proceeds to admire a kind of "research" which is "the greatest possible remove from the usual English stylist's trend or urge toward a style different from everyone else's."

> Anatole France is said to have spent a great deal of time searching for the *least possible* variant that would turn the most

9. Ezra Pound, *Literary Essays of Ezra Pound* (London: Faber and Faber, 1954), p. 286.
10. *Ibid.*, p. 34.

worn-out and commonest phrases of journalism into something distinguished.

Such research is sometimes termed "classicism."[11]

As the translator, sculptor, stylist, and resuscitator of the "dead arts" of verse, Pound felt, I believe, an affinity with Landor's "hardness" — which appears to be not simply good style, but a hard reliance upon *style itself*. Comparing *il maestro* with Milton, Hugh Kenner defines the Landor-like ideal of profundity as an aspect of style, and of ethics as an aspect of tone:

> Nothing is commoner than the supposition that Pound's intense concern for the craft of verse marks a separation between form and content, technique and sensibility (journalist's version: "he can only translate"). So it is not surprising that the revaluation of Milton with which his name is connected should be thought of as occurring at the level of technique alone, the only level at which Pound is supposed to work. But the dichotomy between myth and treatment belongs to the Miltonic ethos and not to the Poundian.[12]

That is, Pound writes as one confident that profundity is treatment; he is also, in some of his many modes as a poet, like Landor in preferring a "way of writing," or traditional voice, to any attempt at the idiom of contemporary speech. When Pound does use modern speech it is dramatically, in quotation marks, as a dialect or "way of writing" of its own, and the repeated emphasis of his criticism is upon the voice, not upon speech. As Pound says in relation to Landor's "Dirce," a poet "preferring 'a manner of writing' to the living language, runs considerable danger if he have not a culture as thorough as Landor's."[13] And, there is an encyclopedic quality to the work of both men.

But the use of old story and of history should not be confused with the essential value of "thorough culture" to Landor's verse or to Pound's. To make an only temporarily useful dis-

11. Pound, *ABC of Reading*, p. 70.
12. Hugh Kenner, "New Subtlety of Eyes," *Ezra Pound*, ed. Peter Russell (London: Peter Nevill Limited, 1950), p. 99.
13. Pound, *ABC of Reading*, p. 185.

tinction, history is most valuable as an element of tone, not of subject, to the poet; Pound's or Landor's knowledge of a certain body of excellent writing, historically arranged, lends depth and serious elegance to the poet's style, and the treatment of ancient myth or medieval history is incidental to this poetic means of "containing history." Indeed, the details of myth or fact in Pound often crowd together for want of a truly organizing historical sense, and this effect makes a limpid stylistic surface seem obscure. Landor in this sense knew what he thought about the myths and events which he treated, and so had no such problem; he dealt with certain human passions, not with theories of economic and cultural determinism.

In any case, the historical sense may or may not be used to treat "history"; far more important than Landor's use of a classical plot or an "original" is the tone which suggests the presence of such an original. "Thorough culture" enables a writer to effect this suggestion, to a varying and controlled extent, of a voice more resonant than that of any particular moment of history; as an overtone, this voice can contribute to a tone which is nevertheless personal. On the technical level, the poet of thorough culture can, for example, use grammatical inversions in an authoritative, and therefore acceptably graceful way. He understands when such devices are rhetorically credible, he knows how and when they were idiomatic in several languages, and so he can use supposedly archaic or decorative devices in the service of plain simplicity. The pursuit is to find subjects for which the writing may be idiomatic by being timeless:

> *From Alcaeus*
> *Wormwood and rue be on his tongue*
> *And ashes on his head,*
> *Who chills the feast and checks the song*
> *With emblems of the dead!*
>
> *By young and jovial, wise and brave,*
> *Such mummers are derided.*
> *His sacred rites shall Bacchus have*
> *Unspared and undivided.*

> *Coucht by my friends, I fear no mask*
> *Impending from above,*
> *I only fear the later flask*
> *Which keeps me from my love.*

Pericles and Aspasia *CXXXI* [14]

We can say that a conservative symmetry in the relation of line and caesura with grammar helps to make the grammatical inversions of the first two stanzas "right" and that this effect is helped by the tuneful reemphasis of accent by quantity in the fourth and eighth syllables of the tetrameter lines, in which the inversions, along with most of the inflected verbs, appear. The "half lines" so defined, like the trimeter lines, are rhythmically fluid, and as units, grammatically simple. The rhymes are crisp. The diction is fresh, but derived from that one- or two-syllable area of the language where the plain and the elegant meet. We can add that the most marked grammatical inversion, in the seventh line, serves the slightly increased formality of the quasi-religious invocation which the line suggests. But even this describable element of the poem's success is much easier to write about than to write. We must say, in Pound's manner, that the man just knew what he was doing.

Often, as with the poem above, the actual history becomes a playful foil for the history-as-tone; throughout *Pericles and Aspasia* the prose context presents Greek lyrics of the Periclean Age and earlier, conceived and written, in fact, by W. S. Landor. Thus, in good Poundian manner, Landor offers poems — obviously "original" in the sense being advocated — which are either superb translations or superb English songs, we cannot tell which until we look them up. That it makes no difference, in this genre (actually, they are always Landor's), is part of the civilizing assertion of the tone.

Also in keeping with certain ambitions of Pound's own work

14. Walter Savage Landor, *The Complete Works of Walter Savage Landor*, ed. T. Earle Welby (prose, vols. 1–13) and Stephen Wheeler (poems, vols. 13–16), 16 vols. (London: Chapman and Hall Ltd., 1927–36), 10:123. All of my references to Landor's prose and verse, unless otherwise noted, are based on this edition. From now on I cite from the poems without footnotes.

is Landor's frequent treatment of nineteenth-century celebrities, as well as Periclean ones, in prose and epigrams. This capacity, in the *Imaginary Conversations*, for example, ranges in a single, gracious medium from "Aesop and Rhodope" to the equivalent of, say, "Kasavubu and Picasso."

Without pausing now for further examples, it is enough to say that the value of such work is its tacit declaration that one can devise an historic, timeless tone for a given subject. This accomplishment adorns and strengthens literature even if the experience treated is, as in "Wormwood and Rue," rather small. The formulation of that experience enlarges it by producing a little object-lesson in conceptual dignity. Such a pursuit is largely irrelevant to the modern, almost orthodox, emphasis upon the idioms of "normal speech." This emphasis too may be considered Poundian, but I think that it is for great range in an opposite stylistic direction that Pound honors Landor, and not for mere encyclopedic breadth: "A set of Landor's collected works will go further towards civilizing a man than any university education now on the market."[15]

Donald Davie

Davie writes admirably about compositional elements which are really "in" poems: one of his books is on syntax in English poetry,[16] and another (in which "Landor's Shorter Poems" is the final chapter) is simply called *Purity of Diction in English Verse.* In the first paragraph of his chapter on Landor, Davie says:

> At a crucial stage in the English poetic tradition he [Landor] struck out alone a path of interesting and sensible experiment; and in deciding what chance there was of success, and where

15. Pound, *Literary Essays*, p. 344.
16. Donald Davie, *Articulate Energy: An Enquiry into the Syntax of English Poetry* (New York: Harcourt, Brace and Co., 1958).

and how the experiment failed, we touch upon matters of importance for the writing of poetry at any time.[17]

Landor is compared with Carew, and it is argued that a poet endeavoring to write urbanely, on the basis of rhetorical commonplaces, requires an *urbs*, a community like Carew's. The argument is summarized in the last paragraph of book and essay:

> It [Landor's career] is interesting and important chiefly because his attempt to put the clock back shows how inevitable was the Romantic revolution in poetic method and the conception of the poet's function. . . . To make poetry out of traditional commonplace or personal compliment the poet had to write in and for a homogeneous society acknowledging strong and precise traditions of literature and manners. His awareness of such a society as his audience gave the poet the sureness of tone which comes out of a pure diction and achieves urbanity. When Landor attempted this, all the odds were against him. No such society and no such audience existed . . . Landor is the type of the poet who refuses to acknowledge the temper of his age.[18]

Landor, that is, sought to inspire rhetorical occasions — rather than discoveries. He sought urbane diction, but the only sort of urbanity which Davie finds possible in the nineteenth century is that of Shelley.

Shelley is "the only English Romantic poet with the birth and breeding of a gentleman, and that cannot be irrelevant."[19] To find obscurity or lack of interest in Shelley's "vast metaphors with the human term left out" is "not a mistake only but a social blunder."[20] Shelley's demi-metaphors civilize by gentlemanly urbanity, a quality which Davie finds to be unaccountably most prominent in Shelley's least ambitious poems.

The argument as Davie presents it is brilliant, but its weak point is Shelley, to whom Davie turns almost perversely, it seems at first, in a search for "urbanity." The example of "trium-

17. Davie, *Purity of Diction in English Verse*, p. 183.
18. *Ibid.*, pp. 195–96.
19. *Ibid.*, p. 156.
20. *Ibid.*

phantly successful" diction given is an aspic of slack, genteel Romantic clichés, language which begs such plebeian questions as, how *does* a spirit sit? What *is* it about the way stars scatter light? How does might *exceed* an organ, even an obscure one? ("Eyes" would make better sense with "obscure," though not better idiom.)

> *Whether the Sensitive Plant, or that*
> *Which within its boughs like a Spirit sat,*
> *Ere its outward form had known decay,*
> *Now felt this change, I cannot say.*
>
> *Whether that Lady's gentle mind,*
> *No longer with the form combined,*
> *Which scattered love, as stars do light,*
> *Found sadness, where it left delight,*
>
> *I dare not guess; but in this life*
> *Of error, ignorance, and strife,*
> *Where nothing is, but all things seem,*
> *And we the shadows of the dream,*
>
> *It is a modest creed, and yet*
> *Pleasant if one considers it,*
> *To own that death itself must be,*
> *Like all the rest, a mockery.*
>
> *That garden sweet, that lady fair,*
> *And all sweet shapes and odours there,*
> *In truth have never passed away:*
> *'Tis we, 'tis ours are changed; not they.*
>
> *For love, and beauty, and delight,*
> *There is no death nor change: their might*
> *Exceeds our organs, which endure*
> *No light, being themselves obscure.*

Davie says that no phrase here would be out of place in unaffected prose, but the twelfth line would be in place only in a telegram. "Outward form," "gentle mind," "garden sweet," and "lady fair" (to say nothing of lines 10 and 21) are unaffected because they do not pretend to be other than unambitious clichés; in Davie's other example of triumphant urbanity, from "Julian and Maddalo," the mad speaker remains enough of a sane, carelessly sublime Romantic poeticizer to use these same adjectives: "sweet Venice," "statues fair," "the green country," "the winter night" (rhyming of course with "firelight"), the "dawning day," a lamp which is "alight," and so forth.

Yet Davie is right within his own terms. One suspects that what he really likes about these lines is their close relation, not to prose, but to speech. Landor's urbanity is the artificial one of prose letters; Shelley's is that of conversation, the natural conversation of aesthetically minded nineteenth-century gentlemen. His easy rhymes (strife-life, dream-seem, light-delight, and the many rhymes on pronouns or the verb "to be") exemplify the use of rhyme as a token of the facile, rapid composer, the relaxed man, not as a discipline of the sculptor. "I cannot say," he murmurs, "I dare not guess," "Pleasant if one considers it" (which consideration the poet just barely does give, between philosophic sips of sherry, perhaps), "In truth" — old fellow — "have never passed away." The impression is of urbane, sensitive, careless spontaneity — and Davie quotes the introductory stanzas to "The Witch of Atlas," where Shelley claims just such a quality, as opposed to the stodgy professionalism of "Peter Bell."

Landor's urbanity is literary, not conversational: it consists in restoring life to the conventional language of letters, not to the conversational cliché. We can take, for an example of this tradition, a very simple one from another poet.

> *The gentle reader loves the gentle muse,*
> *That little dares, and little means,*
> *Who humbly sips her learning from Reviews,*
> *And flutters in the Magazines.*

David Garrick (!) writes the stanza with studied rhyme and with a "literary" vocabulary which demonstrates how such a vocabulary should be used. The irony is that of professionalism, not of amateurism. This is Landor's tradition, whatever we may think of Shelley. That Garrick's stanza bears no good or bad mark of a particular *urbs* should be of importance to the modern poet; conventional diction is a means of avoiding the merely poetic diction of a time and place. The stanza bears none of the obstruction which one might find in many lines of, say, Gray; insofar as this is true, Garrick has made a very important achievement. His lines show a coherent, undated attitude toward an aspect of civilization which has persisted from the birth of a certain kind of literary culture to yesterday. My interest in Landor is partly based upon a conviction that modern poetry is extremely standardized in language largely because of a retreat from "written" diction and syntax.

But Davie is interested in a poetry which finds the tone or substance of wisdom in speech, and his two favorites among Landor's epigrams reveal this interest. I find the poems to be among Landor's worst by Landor's normal standards. The prejudice in favor of speech-idiom is so-conventional a part of post–World War II poetic diction that we almost forget that it is a prejudice. Yet no such thing is forgotten by Davie, many of whose poems are very skillful models in the use of such idiom. Furthermore, he isolates such matters in a thoughtful, concise prose, which I will quote at some length:

> At any rate, Landor occasionally makes discoveries of the Wordsworthian sort, not "what oft was thought but ne'er so well expressed," but what was never consciously thought before, nor ever expressed. Even here, I think, he tries more often than he succeeds. But sometimes he can make genuine discoveries, especially about movements of the mind:
>
> > *Something (ah! tell me what) there is*
> > *To cause that melting tone.*
> > *I fear a thought has gone amiss*
> > *Returning quite alone.*
>
> In this field, urbanity is of no account, as the name of Wordsworth may remind us. For it is achievement of this sort which preserves many of Wordsworth's early poems, where the diction is eccentric and the versification barely adequate. So, in the poem quoted, the diction of the first two lines is faded and decadent, but this is important only because it leads us to expect something quite different from what we are given thereafter. In other words, it makes the discovery more sudden and surprising. Perhaps for this reason, the lines have been found obscure, but their bearing is plain enough. Landor catches in a touching metaphor the experience of breaking off a line of

thought, surprised by a melancholy reflection. He explains the shadow falling across the face of his companion by the supposition that a thought has "gone amiss" (i.e., broken off the train of thought of which it was a link) and "returned alone," or, as the common metaphor has it, "brought home" to the thinker a melancholy truth. The poem, one could say, is an exploration and a discovery of what we mean when we say "The truth was brought home to me." To give form to an experience so fugitive yet so permanently human seems to me an achievement of a high order. Unfortunately I can think of only one other case in which Landor does something comparable, in his poem "For an Urn in Thoresby Park."[21]

One way of reading Landor is here defined: the "discoveries" are few, for he normally worked, as to subject, away from discovery — and, as to diction, away from the only possible urbanity (that is, the speech) of his *urbs*.

This position is similar to that of Pound, and of this book, in everything but its evaluation of Landor's success. Davie is now about to suffer the penalty for his excellence as a writer: his work is not only excellent but useful as well, and I am about to attempt a description of Davie's own context in literary history. Unfortunately the problem which I have in mind is rather a cliché regarding his generation of young poets. I will try, nonetheless, to keep my simplifications fair.

Donald Davie (b. 1922) is a distinguished member of the decidedly post-revolutionary, post-Poundian generation which is presently looking, in various directions, for a way to "make it new." Quite unlike Pound, Davie does not, in this search, take the tone of one bursting with the secret of how to write. His poetry has, over his career, changed considerably; it sometimes treats these changes, and in a tone more reflective than Poundian-assertive:

> *The metaphysicality*
> *Of poetry, how I need it!*
> *And yet it was for years*
> *What I refused to credit.*
> from "Or, Solitude," New Statesman, *December 30, 1965*

21. *Ibid.*, pp. 194–95.

So with poetics: never a revolution
But has its mould. Look, in the overturning
Approaching comber, rolling inside out,
A roof of cream moves back through a mounting wall.
    from "*Bolyai, the Geometer,*" Events and Wisdoms, *1964*

For such a theme (atrocities) you find
My style, you say, too neat and self-possessed.
    from "*Method, for Ronald Gaskell,*" Brides of Reason, *1955*

You may be right. "How can I dare to feel?"
May be the only question I can pose.
     from "*Rejoinder to a Critic,*" A Winter Talent, *1957*

Davie grants that he changes, that revolutions cannot be total, and that the other fellow "may be right" about style. This modesty is countered by a fierce regard for subject matter and for the importance of the poetic function — even if no style seems to fulfill that function perfectly.

Davie's criticism also suggests that "how to write," which was a starting point for Pound and Landor, is for him a search — and, that this search points in at least some ways away from Pound (*qua* anti-Romantic) and toward Wordsworth. In a chapter entitled "What Is Modern Poetry?"[22] this direction, and its corollary skepticism about Landor's kind of experiment, are plain. The chapter compares Pound's "The Gypsy" with Wordsworth's "Stepping Westward," and states what seems to me to be quite true of these two poems: "it is difficult to deny that Pound's is much superior."[23] Difficult indeed, but Davie finally does deny it. Pound's poem, it is shown, is better written rhythmically, as to concision, and otherwise "*as a poem.*" *Sic.* Wordsworth's poem, however, "is more original than Pound's," for Pound's poem is merely a (Landorian, for my purposes) perfection of tone in relation to a certain experience, while Wordsworth's poem discovers a new sentiment about a similar subject:

> That there is a wistfulness at the heart of the wanderlust is no new idea; and that need not matter when the old idea is expressed so memorably as it is by Pound. But Wordsworth's rec-

22. Davie, *Articulate Energy*, pp. 154–60.
23. *Ibid.* p. 155.

ognition that the wanderlust is acknowledged by traditional sentiment, and that that acknowledgment makes it all the more attractive — that is the sort of idea that could have occurred only to Wordsworth; it is something far more strange and novel.[24]

So much, in other words, for the projects of Landor's career. Landor's "discoveries about human sentiment" *are* his poems, the words, commas, and lines of his poems, the tones which he gives us in response to "the old idea." Wordsworth's discoveries show us the actual, sociological, or personal extent and force of a commonplace. Clearly, there are two kinds of poetry in question, and these kinds have at least some relevance to modern poetry.

Now, I obviously disagree with Davie about the degree of Landor's success and about the relation of a poet to his age and audience; it would be a particularly shabby kind of argument *ad hominem* if in the course of presuming to "explain" Davie's position I should surreptitiously argue against it. And so I will conclude by explaining some of the differences which, later, I will argue by example.

I think that poets tend to be "determined" by their age less than other men, and that the best poets almost by definition are most free from the temper of the age. I think that Landor, like most poets, wrote for other poets — dead, living, and potential. As an example to support this point of view, the aristocratic wits, bluestockings, and amateurs of the Augustan period present a most homogeneous audience which knew very well what it wanted; this audience, with its prestige, power, and confidence, presented at the very least as many difficulties and restrictions for poets as it lent advantages. The poetry of the period is notable for a broad range of subject treated with a notoriously small range of tones (thus the "mock"-this and -that). This is very far from the kind of lyric which Landor sought. His voice was meant to suggest the voice of a certain, historically vertical civilization, modified by the voice of W. S. Landor, not the voice of an age or place.

24. *Ibid.*, p. 157.

If the epigram by Carew which Davie quotes [25] is superior to the Landor poems with which Davie compares it, certainly the margin is not striking.

Carew :   *To her, whose beauty doth excell*
             Stories, we tosse theis cupps, and fill
             Sobrietie, a sacrifice
       To the bright lustre of her eyes.
       Each soul that sipps this is divine:
       Her beauty deifies the wine.

Landor: *Stand close around, ye Stygian set,*
             With Dirce in one boat conveyed!
       Or Charon, seeing, may forget
       That he is old and she a shade.

Landor: *Past ruin'd Ilion Helen lives,*
             Alcestis rises from the shades;
       Verse calls them forth; 'tis verse that gives
       Immortal youth to mortal maids.

       Soon shall Oblivion's deepening veil
             Hide all the peopled hills you see,
       The gay, the proud, while lovers hail
       These many summers you and me.

For me, the conjunction of these poems illustrates primarily that Carew in at least one poem did indeed speak to a certain extent in the voice of Caroline England, and that Landor in at least two poems spoke with a voice deliberately as removed as possible from any particular place and time. Most of Landor's poems strive, by inventing small, potent variations from the expected, to achieve just such a voice. Therefore, a particular society and its homogeneity or dissociation are irrelevancies; Landor, in other words, never exactly realized that he was "obstinate," "wrong-headed," or even an experimenter in the sense which Davie intends. He merely was trying what seemed clear ways, the main ways, to better writing. I think that this conclusion is supported by what we know of Landor's opinions; he thought that his poetry was above all clear at a time when most poets seemed to pursue other virtues, inconsistent with clarity.

25. *Ibid.*, p. 157.

But as to nineteenth-century society, my impression is that on the whole Landor (apart from his radical politics) found it slightly less worthy of his serious attention than the several other societies with which he was familiar. But this question is complicated, and Landor was a violently complex man.

The fact is that I find Landor's shortcomings — a sentimental carelessness of thought, the exploitation of emotion for its own sake — similar to the shortcomings of his contemporaries. He is at his best an exemplar and spokesman for a certain attitude toward the past. Connected with this attitude is the idea that originality consists in the use — not even necessarily the radical "invention" — of style; he failed when he drifted with his age, not when he rebelled against it.

Yet sometimes, for the space of a few lines, he could anticipate Pound by altogether ceasing to think, or at least seeming to do so by allowing his ear for diction, syntax, and rhythm to, far outstrip the rigor of his thought. Thus, in his "The Album Opened,"

> *Just as opposite in merit*
> *As in place these lines you see.*
> *She has pathos, she has spirit,*
> *Naught but what she gives has he.*
>
> *Never image springs without her,*
> *Rose comes first, and last comes Rose,*
> *And the chaff he throws about her*
> *Her bright amber drops enclose.*

the poem seems at first to display rediscovered the Renaissance belief in, and power over, abstract diction. "Merit," "place," "pathos," "spirit," and "opposite" seem, like the self-descriptive sixth line, to have special and almost technical significance. Wit, and the mind's categories, appear to have the life and conviction which such diction bears in Shakespeare's "The Phoenix and the Turtle," Marvell's "The Definition of Love," or the great and noble "Elegy on the Death of Sidney," variously attributed but probably by Fulke Greville:

> *Place, pensive, wails his fall whose presence was her pride.*

Yet, the longer we look at Greville's lines, the more they mean, while Landor's meaning shimmers and escapes. His poem is a façade of bright style which suggests more framework than is there. He could hear the *tone* of belief in abstraction, but he did not really have that belief. Entirely aside from Greville's more serious subject, Landor's poem lacks almost entirely the compression and substance which Greville establishes with his memorable first line:

> *Silence augmenteth grief, writing increaseth rage.*

But one would have to look very carefully, and try to paraphrase Landor's poem, to detect its fraud — its "pure" style. The poem is not in the mode of his best work, but while defining certain of Landor's limitations, "The Album Opened" also demonstrates the superb ear for tone which is in other poems his great strength.

In any case, Landor's career seems especially pertinent to the definition of two kinds of poetry: poetry which emphasizes the discovery of content and poetry which emphasizes the discovery of tone. Clearly, this division signifies two ways toward one end. The matter is not very simple, but it supplies a fruitful ground for argument. The Poundian idea of "thorough culture" as a way of writing is, for instance, a potential argument against those who consider Pound (or Eliot) to be automatically greater than Wallace Stevens because Stevens does not "contain history."

The study of Landor's poems will from now on define my exploration of what can become a maze of literary-historical speculations. But if there is any justice at all in the idea of Landor as a poet's poet, then an awareness of still current polarities in poetic theory should offer a suitable entry into his work.

The Rhetorical Donnée:
Commonplace, Myth, and Occasion

Introductory

I shall now try (after a few more generalities) to follow Landor's
pertinent advice by discussing some particular lines and poems.
I begin with some very brief and perhaps inconsiderable-look-
ing poems in order to illustrate certain preliminary points com-
pactly and by extreme examples.

Partly because he did not need the space, the sheer length,
which is often required by a poem which pretends to literal,
as well as stylistic, discovery, Landor had available to him as
a form the epigram:

> *On love, on grief, on every human thing,*
> *Time sprinkles Lethe's water with his wing.*

The definition of "commonplace" suitable to my purpose is "a
reclaimable truism," and this excellent epigram on oblivion is

indeed based upon a most banal truism which Landor does, I think, reclaim. The lines move the reader an appropriate part of the way toward tears, and they do so not by directly claiming, implying, or even pretending any particular experience of the old truth. The "experience," in the sense of the poet's personal encounter with the old truth, is assumed or ignored; yet, "Lethe" is not a cliché, but a poem.

Furthermore, the poem is not a seventeenth-century epigram, but discernibly a nineteenth-century one, and it is of Landor, colored by his own somewhat sentimental stoicism. Although the couplet may recall Jonson or Herrick, neither of those poets would have used such diction as the casual "thing" or the general, unqualified "love." And, Herrick might have conceived the delicate physical action of the last line for Cupid, but not for Time.

A two-line poem, then, reinspires a commonplace, remains at the level of the general, and displays a peculiar tonal coloring which probably explains the successful reinspiration. To understand that process in "Lethe" one must attend to the details of style which give the statement emotional credence: the nature of the rhyme (fresh, witty without frivolity), the role of monosyllabic and disyllabic words, the effect of pauses within the line, the distribution of grammatical elements, and so forth. In other words, it is necessary to reclaim by a special attention our own clichés about Landor's Classicism, returning to Pound's definition, which bears repeating:

> the *least possible* variant that would turn the most worn-out and commonest phrases of journalism into something distinguished. Such research is sometimes termed "classicism."[1]

It should be added that such a pursuit restores the life and flesh of old formulations; it does not merely refurbish them verbally. "Lethe" is not good "because" of a successful rhyme, skillful pauses, and a happy figure of speech; it is good because those stylistic successes conduct us to an emotional comprehen-

---

1. Ezra Pound, *ABC of Reading* (New York: New Directions, 1960), p. 70.

sion of a certain idea about life. That the resources used include least possible variants is not a technical embellishment, but a vital part of the emotion: that the poem's truth can be said in two lines enables the poet to bear that truth with containment.

At the same time, Landor is not so "un-Romantic" and anomalous a figure in his age as he has sometimes been painted. In many ways, certainly, his work thwarts or evades certain expectations about nineteenth-century poetry. In addition, some of Landor's goals and procedures especially disappoint those of our expectations about all poetry which are most clearly inherited from the nineteenth century. Yet, in manner and subject, few lines of Landor are not very much of their age; the elusive spirit of anomaly originates not in the given text, but off the page, in the man's whole way of working — in his method.

As a result, because Landor's poems deal with the subjects of his major contemporaries, but from a different, isolated idea of what a subject is, his poetry is too often treated as undiscussable. (Or, worse, as "insincere," as though he tried to pass himself off as a "genuine" Romantic.)

It would be foolish and presumptuous to apologize in such a way for Landor's solitary position, for he is a strong and beautiful poet. Rather, one should begin by explaining the difficulties which Landor's method causes for an understanding of his achievement. By method, I mean the poet's assumptions, determinations, and strategies in relation to concepts like "unity," "subject," or "profundity." In vital ways, Landor's terms often had meanings slightly different from those we know, and his concepts, different references. This allegiance to a vocabulary and to aesthetic values partly outside the succeeding course and need of history, perhaps defines the great "minor" poet. Certainly in Landor's case neither the reach for a great subject nor the grasp of an original style was modest. Far from ignoring the idea of greatness, or of originality, he had particular, perhaps unexpected conceptions of those qualities:

> A poet of the first order must have formed, or taken to himself and modified, some great subject. He must be creative and con-

structive. [I.e., capable of constructing.] Creativeness may work upon old materials: a new world may spring from an old one. Shakespeare found Hamlet and Ophelia; he found Othello and Desdemona; nevertheless he, the only universal poet, carried this, and all the other qualifications, far beyond the reach of competitors. . . .[2]

That creativeness may work upon old materials can serve as a guide to understanding Landor's poetic method.

Above all, he wrote well and intended to delight; caring little for what he called "metaphysics," Landor cared profoundly about the details of sentence, word, and rhythm. To say this is close to the familiar, hollow praise of Landor as a "great stylist" whose thoughts and perceptions — it is implied — are of no interest. Although in a limited way true, that cliché obscures Landor's peculiar successes and failings.

I propose that those successes and failings are stylistic, and that the lovely, distinctive way of writing which is often described as Landor's "classical style," linked somehow with his impressive Latin scholarship, arises in fact from a particular method, or attitude toward poem writing. The nature of this method, and its importance in understanding Landor's work, are not such speculative matters as they might seem; the evidence is in the "contents of the book," in the decisions implied by each poem.

Briefly, Landor's procedure is to revitalize, through profound energies of understanding and a cleanly exactitude of style, an already established situation or observation. Stylistic perfection in the work, then, demonstrates the degree to which the chosen commonplace has been comprehended, and the skill of thought so demonstrated is personal and original.

Such formal achievements in language are of course worthy of intellectual respect; the poetic and intellectual tradition in question informs the great poetry of the sixteenth and seventeenth centuries. But Landor did not write in the age of Donne,

2. Walter Savage Landor, *The Complete Works of Walter Savage Landor*, ed. T. Earle Welby, and Stephen Wheeler, 16 vols. (London: Chapman and Hall Ltd., 1927–36), 11:222.

Herbert, and Jonson, and his career raises the special problem toward which my examinations of particular poems are addressed: the difficulties and advantages for a poet whose procedure resembles one which had begun to be abandoned well before the time of Young, and whose milieu is the age of Wordsworth. Aside from the area of composition, moreover, his thought is decidedly of that milieu.

If we so view Landor, as a man trying to write within a disappearing tradition of the poet as reflective artisan, we gain this: our judgments of his poems will not be of "sincerity" and "insincerity," but of successful and unsuccessful writing.

It is true, of course, that Landor's contemporaries sometimes adapted stereotyped subjects or attitudes, often deliberately. But in such a case, I think, a theoretical "typical" Romantic writer works within the convention that his theme originates in his particular experience. His poem creates an illusion that the sentiment or incident *occurred to* the poet, on a nonliterary level common to all men. In the Romantic convention of composition, the proper style, the true tone of understanding, follows naturally and without elaborate adjustment from the authentic experience, couched in the suitable language of nature. To write "in a convention," as I understand it, means that the writer proceeds as though certain things were true; as its own base, the poem suggests these conventional assumptions to the reader.

Thus, when Landor and Wordsworth each write a Romantic poem within a very traditional motif, the enormous difference is in the manner of speaking. The manner of speaking in turn indicates two distinct conceptions of what a poem is.

For example, the correspondence of the poet's emotional state with the time of year is, entirely apart from the so-called pathetic fallacy, a basic and traditional kind of poem. Poets have for centuries naturally celebrated *reverdis* or lamented the year's decline. For Wordsworth, the general nature of the season, actual or traditional, is tacit; he presents a particular scene, at a particular instant:

> *When all at once I saw a crowd,*
> *A host, of golden daffodils. . . .*

And most of his poem is devoted to a skillful description, not only of the seaside field of daffodils, but of the experiencing of them in a few moments. Wordsworth carefully defines his reaction as an inevitable part of the scene,

> *A poet could not but be gay,*
> *In such a jocund company;*
> *I gazed — and gazed — but little thought*
> *What wealth the show to me had brought. . . .*

And the poem's greatest level of generality, in the concluding stanza, detaches the immediate experience from the generality, which in fact consists of the recreation in reverie of that original, particular moment:

> *For oft, when on my couch I lie,*
> *They flash upon that inward eye*
> *Which is the bliss of solitude;*
> *And then my heart with pleasure fills,*
> *And dances with the daffodils.*

Conventions surrounding flowers or springtime may pertain to this poem, but they are of slight relevance. The poem's meaning and style depend utterly upon our conventional acceptance of the experience as authentic and particular. It does not matter that Wordsworth did, one day, see the daffodils; we are in any case quite willing to pretend or assume that "he," in the poem, did.

Landor begins his poem on autumn with two increasingly general statements:

> *The leaves are falling; so am I; . . .*

"The" leaves have none of the urgent particularity of the daffodils. The next lines of the poem furnish a specific descriptive detail, but the air of wittily straightforward generalization continues:

> *The few late flowers have moisture in the eye;*
> *So have I too.*

> *Scarcely on any bough is heard*
> *Joyous, or even unjoyous, bird*
> *The whole wood through.*
> *Winter may come: he brings but nigher*
> *His circle (yearly narrowing) to the fire*
> *Where old friends meet:*
> *Let him; now heaven is overcast,*
> *And spring and summer both are past,*
> *And all things sweet.*

The wit, the apparent simplicity, the gentle mockery of himself, of his dewy eye, and of convention ("or even unjoyous") are all eminently *conscious* in tone. They suggest a man who is almost unbearably aware of what he is doing. Conscious, too, is the blatantly explicit way in which the comparison of man and nature is conducted.

Yet despite the explicitness and the simplicity, the poem is elegant and complex, a melancholy foreboding of the withdrawal from consciousness forever. Only Landor's specialized taste could have successfully written the boldly unadorned opening (or closing) of the poem. The circle of friends, too, will be neither joyous nor unjoyous, and the bitter welcoming of them and of winter is the farthest thing from conventional in the pejorative sense.

The daring and poignancy of Landor's plainness are conventional, however, in that they depend upon our understanding that the statement could easily have been banal. Certain obvious conventions about the seasons are crucially relevant — while the literal authenticity of the leaves and flowers clearly does not matter.

Even Landor's speaker is authentic only in a way and to a degree — similarly to the speaker of

> *Western wind, when will thou blow,*
> *The small rain down can rain?*
> *Christ, if my love were in my arms*
> *And I in my bed again!*

Winds and seasons have significant conventional associations. We accept the experience as real in its general essence rather than in literal detail, and we are persuaded to do so by an effect of the exact words.

In other words, Wordsworth's lyric is in somewhat closer relationship to fiction. But the comparison also could be made between (more or less) narrative poems by each man. In "Resolution and Independence" the fictive illusion is of an utterly authentic, personal, and particular experience. From this unique event — a conversation with an old man who gathers leeches — a poem follows. And through the poem's twenty stanzas, the poem's movement, and the narrator's state of mind, and the conversation, all move in a line. The emotional persuasiveness of incident and visual detail is frequently asserted, and the unique objective event thus appears to have an irresistible emotional analogue. This feeling, unlike the particular leech-gatherer, is presented as something universal. If the Romantic poet is the man who discovers the inherently perfect words for feeling, then, in the Wordsworthian convention, the poem itself originated in the incident. Universal to all mankind and (it is pretended) in a way preexistent, the poem is not at all original, in the most literal sense, to a particular intellect.

Nearly opposite in convention, Landor's *Hellenics* intend an agreement between poet and reader that the characters and situations represent a commonplace of external origin. Rhetorically, this is true even of the invented plot elements in the *Hellenics*. The poems imply that Landor chose certain situations for study, and that after he had applied himself to them they became his own; the product and the evidence of this assimilation are there, in the art of Landor's language. The tone, the precise psychological effect of the style, embodies Landor's creative effort. The style is his proof that he has wrested a device — the commonplace — to the condition of a statement.

An interesting clarification of the preceding idea is provided by M. H. Abrams in *The Mirror and the Lamp*. Abrams points out that in Wordsworth's essay *Upon Epitaphs* the Romantic poet reprimands Dr. Johnson for praising a composition because in it, says Johnson, "there is scarce one line taken from commonplaces." Wordsworth defends the commonplace — not as a time-tried means by which a poet may achieve the serious treatment of a coherent subject, but because it is

> a primary requisite in an epitaph that it shall contain thoughts and feelings which are in their substance commonplace . . . it is grounded upon the universal intellectual property of man, — sensations which all men have felt and feel daily and hourly. . . . But it is required that these truths should be in-stinctively ejaculated or should rise irresistably from circum-stances.[3]

That is, Wordsworth defines the commonplace only as it signifies a common human reaction to experience *in "substance"* — not at all as a literary, formal device by which the poet masters personal material. The "art" implicitly recommended is the art of supplying the reader with a patently authentic, immediate cause for the commonplace, irresistible, and circumstantial.

The difference in Landor's emphasis, when proposing a simi-lar idea, is very great, as revealed by the metaphor which he chooses:

> Nothing in poetry is original. The best poets have always labored with the same conceptions. . . . The clashing of characters brought out those sparks in Shakespeare which will be unextin-guished in the breast of millions to all eternity. Men before him have thought and felt somewhat of the same. There was earth before God moulded it into man.[4]

The commonplace is not the ejaculated or rising breath; it is unmolded earth.

As to the literal authenticity of feeling for which Words-worth appears to argue, we can refer to an exchange between Boccaccio and Petrarca in Landor's *Pentameron*. In this work as in the *Imaginary Conversations*, it is safe to assume that all energetic characters who are not priests or Frenchmen speak

---

3. M. H. Abrams, *The Mirror and the Lamp* (Oxford: Oxford University Press, 1953), p. 62.

4. Stephen Wheeler, *Letters and Other Unpublished Writings of Walter Savage Landor* (London: Duckworth and Co., 1899), p. 62.

for the author; in the person of Boccaccio, Landor, a pure Romantic in so many other matters, here shocks us with a home truth about literary composition. The important thing to notice is Boccaccio's cooperative attitude as a reader:

> Boccaccio: Frequently, where there is great power in poetry, the imagination makes encroachments on the heart, and uses it as her own. I have shed tears on writings which never cost the writer a sigh, but which occasioned him to rub his hands together until they were ready to strike fire, with satisfaction at having overcome the difficulty of being tender.
>
> Petrarca: Giovanni! Are you not grown satirical?
>
> Boccaccio: Not in this. It is a truth as broad and glaring as the eye of the cyclops.[5]

The reader, in other words, is to understand that the emotion of the poem — real as it is — exists in its truest, most perfect state on the page, in the tone of the poem. This tone is likely to be the product of many separate, brilliant moments of composition, each fashioning the inert clay of the commonplace. The *exact* emotion is the tone of the poem; unlike the original commonplace, it never existed until the last painstaking revision was completed.

One can say that Landor sees his value as a poet to be that of giving us tones, exact qualities of response to generalized, and therefore familiar experience; he assumes a basic, quite available, and rather vague commonality of human emotion, and he struggles for clarification and definition within this commonality. The definition makes the emotion acute. Wordsworth on the other hand struggles to reach and tap a not-so-available commonality of emotion. Once tapped, the emotion is self-defined and already intense, and it is likely that penetration to such a level will comprise the major part of the poet's work. This procedure implies that there is a single, universal tone adequate to each experience. Wordsworth recalls his reader to the "commonplace" — or, perhaps, to the racial wisdom. The commonplace is for Wordsworth the magnificent end, for

5. Landor, *Works*, 9:247.

Landor, the convenient beginning, the uninspired earth, of poetry.

Such distinctions in matters of conception are perhaps easier to state than to see. The rest of this chapter is organized into a few categories of ascending importance, with examples, for some of Landor's typical subjects and strategies. My object is to show how matters of conception and method can be seen in the work, and how those same matters can clarify the scope of the work.

I begin with "Rose Aylmer" as one of many poems based upon those universal sentiments, wider than genres, which perhaps most closely resemble the commonplace as Wordsworth uses the term. "Rose Aylmer" illustrates how small the changes may be which reclaim the commonplace through authorial awareness.

The second section, on the "Fiesolan Idyl," suggests that Landor sometimes uses Romantic feeling self-consciously, as something separable and acquired — in effect, as a commonplace.

In the third and fourth sections, I approach Landor's extensive use of mythology, trying to characterize the rather neglected *Hellenics* and to contrast them with the overpraised *Chrysaor.*

Finally, in a longer section concluding with the poem "To My Child Carlino," I treat Landor's characteristic approach as it works in his many occasional poems. These poems treat their subjects from the perspective of a special personal situation, very like certain dramatic "places" in the original tradition of the commonplace. Here Landor, as a Romantic artist, turns the subject very markedly toward introspection and personal feeling. The same can be said to some degree of the poems which I discuss within every category; the theme of this chapter is the repeated turning inward of the initial material as it is worked by the combination of a Romantic intelligence and a traditional method of composition.

I should add that these categories are offered as temporarily convenient and indicative. They by no means exhaust or even very satisfactorily arrange Landor's work.

Poems Treating Universal Sentiments

Landor may be best known for poems like the one which begins:

> *Past ruin'd Ilion Helen lives,*
> *Alcestis rises from the shades;*
> *Verse calls them forth; 'tis verse that gives*
> *Immortal life to mortal maids. . . .*

These poems briefly perfect and epitomize some one of those themes which are commonplaces by a quite narrow definition: the lament for a death; the compliment upon excellence of mind, form, or family; the observation of passing time; the celebration of one's mistress. It is remarkable that a nineteenth-century English poet rather than an earlier one should be the maker of so many customary examples of this kind of poem. (How many students think or would think that "Past Ruin'd Ilion Helen Lives" is the work of someone like Nashe, Drayton, or Herrick?) I suspect that this is so partly because our taste in poems is in many ways that of the nineteenth century, and Landor's poems are, in their way, of their time. Consider the slightly overripe stoicism of the following hoary favorite, similar to some of the best stanzas in Edward FitzGerald's *Rubaiyat*:

> *I strove with none, for none was worth my strife:*
> *Nature I loved, and, next to Nature, Art:*
> *I warmed both hands before the fire of Life;*
> *It sinks; and I am ready to depart.*

Landor's relation to his subject in such poems resembles the more exaggerated mode of the pre-Raphaelites and the 'Nineties: an innocent simplicity is rather wistfully idealized through a medium which emphasizes its own sophisticated craft. In short, such poetry is, like "The Leaves Are Falling," self-conscious. But it is through a keen self-consciousness that Landor revitalizes his material, and what is naïve or jaded does not satisfy him. Self-consciousness, if craft be equal to treating it with honest balance, is not a mannerism but a virtue of the understanding; Landor's poems are better than FitzGerald's *Rubaiyat*.

Questions of value aside, Landor's work differs in kind from what might be called the mock-simple or quasi-innocent poem. Although the type begins at least as early as the eighteenth-century vogue for ballads and folk songs, the most immediate association is with the later Romantics, Tennyson in particular, who were fond of simple, traditional themes. "Mariana" and "The Miller's Daughter" embroider traditionally poetic, broadly defined sentiments. Such poems, though, tend to be long and ballad-like, while Landor tends to be epigrammatic and, though perhaps song-like, always inscribed.

Examples from Tennyson and Landor may help to clarify briefly that distinction. Tennyson's "Ode To Memory" is not precisely in the innocent mode, but it does take commonplace sentiments for its conceptual basis. A poem of 124 lines and five sections, it begins:

I
Thou who stealest fire,
From the fountains of the past,
To glorify the present, O, haste
Visit my low desire!
Strengthen me, enlighten me!
I faint in this obscurity,
Thou dewy dawn of memory.

II
Come not as thou camest of late,
Flinging the gloom of yesternight
On the white day, but robed in soften'd light
Of orient state,
Whilome thou camest with the morning mist,
Even as a maid, whose stately brow
The dew-impearled winds of dawn have kissed,
When she. . . .

And so on through further description of the metaphorical maid. In section V, Tennyson lists for twenty or thirty lines a series of landscapes, divided by the word "or," which Memory might recall; the landscapes and the writing are lovely. The poem's conceptual frame, in other words, remains essentially at ground level: the poet's ambition has been to "say it beautifully," so that the untransformed commonplace is forgotten or ignored.

Landor's much shorter poem on memory, which I discuss closely in a later chapter (pp. 128–31), begins by flatly announcing an avowed commonplace. His consciousness of it is part of the conception, and in a comparable number of lines as just quoted from Tennyson, Landor undertakes a considerable redirecting of the commonplace toward the particular:

> *The mother of the Muses, we are taught,*
> *Is Memory; she has left me; they remain,*
> *And shake my shoulder, urging me to sing*
> *About the summer days, my loves of old.*
> *Alas! Alas! is all I can reply.*
> *Memory has left me with that name alone,*
> *Harmonious name, which other bards may sing,*
> *But her bright image in my darkest hour*
> *Comes back, in vain comes back, call'd or uncall'd.*
> *Forgotten are the names. . . .*

The conventional muses are a device not of elaboration but of compression. They economically refer us to a familiar and general sort of statement, similar to Tennyson's, upon which Landor bases a quite particular situation, a special statement. His opening period illustrates the spark of irony which nearly always comes with intense concision. That irony is made explicit in the poem's conclusion, where the rosy reverie is darkened by the reader's discovery that "that name alone" means, not "one name," but *the name only*; thus, the final lines dispel completely the original commonplace, the invocation of pleasant memories:

> *A blessing wert thou, O oblivion,*
> *If thy stream carried only weeds away,*
> *But vernal and autumnal flowers alike*
> *It hurries down to wither on the strand.*

"Memory" is in truth about oblivion, and the poem uses its conventional elements not for copiousness, but to enter efficiently its own special realm.

Tennyson's commonplace remains, by intention, largely in

its received form; his tone is full and ambitious partly because the Tennysonian organ music, as the primary fresh element in the work, is an absolute requirement. That is, the style is inflexible because its first function is decoration. Landor makes us aware that he is beginning with a commonplace; that awareness in his poem transforms the material in a way that is not decorative. Self-consciousness can be elegant and renewing.

As an example of such elegant, renewing self-consciousness, "Rose Aylmer" includes, without cant or muddle, several of the basic sentiments which I listed at the beginning of this category: someone has died; she was excellent in several ways; time takes all things; the poet, personally, admires this lady. It is in a way difficult to notice this inclusiveness or anything else about this anthology-piece because it is so conventional, and so impeccably written. But an examination of the poem's two tonal elements, formality and plainness, will illustrate Landor's method at its most deft and minimal — and will even hint at his major subjects.

> *Ah what avails the sceptred race,*
> *Ah what the form divine!*
> *What every virtue, every grace!*
> *Rose Aylmer, all were thine.*
>
> *Rose Aylmer, whom these wakeful eyes*
> *May weep, but never see,*
> *A night of memories and of sighs*
> *I consecrate to thee.*

The two tonal elements correspond in some degree with the two stanzas, though formality and plainness also coexist in each stanza.

Within the first stanza, the stately movement, the apostrophe, the restrained archaism of diction and syntax, all emphasize the straightforwardness of "virtue" and "grace," without obvious contrast. The archaism is, in essence, not archaism but a careful eschewal of *any* idiom. So conservatively general that it is timeless and in a way bold, the diction of the stanza fulfills certain neoclassic ideals as does very little neoclassic verse. "Timeless" is no cant word: so far as such neutrality is possible, the flavor of these words is of no era, no place, and no personality. In accord with such diction, the relation between grammatical phrase and metrical line in the stanza is plain and rather symmetrical. Even the symmetrical and absolute hyperbole of "every" and "all" is plain as well as formal — modest because it is unaffected.

In short, the stanza is so plain, though in an area where plainness and formality overlap, that one would expect it to fail through flatness. Nevertheless, the four lines constitute decorous, true epitaph, unabashedly final and grave. They lay claim to the voice of worked rock and offer their own tact and authenticity as proof that the subject merits that voice.

The first stanza is in fact cut on Rose Aylmer's gravestone, and it is just to call Landor's style "lapidary." The balance of formality and plainness, which shifts in the second stanza, is sustained in two notable ways. First, "Rose Aylmer" has a distinct cantabile quality. (Charles Lamb chanted it hypnotically, repeatedly, drunk or sober.) The melody springs from a skillful alternation of long and short vowels and from a very fluid movement from syllable to syllable; the single and significant exception to that fluidity is the slight lag on the plosives "weep, but" in the next stanza.

Secondly, "Rose Aylmer," especially in the first stanza, avoids figures, a restraint which helps distinguish the poem from the thousands of artificial album-verses which it resembles and survives. Landor's precise balancing of the formal donnée with personal emotion would, here, be undone by the pat narcissism of a trope, even by the slightest allusion. The principle is relaxed somewhat, along with other elements, in the second stanza, but one can say that few eighteenth-century writers would have ventured to sound so monumental without more figures. In a way, a writer must be sufficiently "Romantic" to claim Landor's rhetoric.

If this last formulation is justified, it is because the all but chilly dignity of these initial four lines is tempered by a sort of dramatic awareness of their own rhetoric, an awareness effected in part by the very compression. Mere, innocent elegiac hyperbole would not be quite so stark and symmetrical in drapery, and Landor's tone is to some small extent, perhaps the extent of the plain but happily lovely English name, put on, assumed from the outset like a ritual garment.

This impression is confirmed by the second quatrain, which is not engraved on Rose Aylmer's stone. The wakeful eyes, still general enough to maintain the poem's decorum, are distinctly particular, personal, and figurative compared to the "sceptered race" and "virtue" of the first stanza; and, again without breaking the procedure of the first quatrain, the enjambment of "eyes/may weep" departs from that procedure. The caesura after "weep" immediately recontains this freer movement, but, as the first caesura to appear unsymmetrically early in the line, and as one between two plosives, this pause also contributes to the delicate shift in tone.

These technical devices enable the poem to undermine smoothly certain conventional expectations. The night of memories and sighs is a remarkable descent from the solemnly incanted superlatives of the first stanza, which might more expectedly precede a stylized lament of all nature, or a lifetime of sighs. And finally, the compact summary at the poem's opening leads us to expect the conventional resolution of personal epitaphs: a consolation. But instead of pieties we have a single night, and for consolation only the grace and sincerity with which the speaker stops short of consolation.[6]

Moreover, withdrawal from the original commonplace's large rhetorical expectations saves "A night of memories and of sighs" from mere melodrama; similarly, the delayed verb of the last line, with a partial return to the more latinate, ritual tone of the poem's beginning, saves the whole stanza from bathos. The interest of the poem, tacitly, is in the speaker's methodical penetration of his subject, Landor's attempt to reconcile the

6. See A. L. Bennett, "The Principal Rhetorical Conventions in the Renaissance Personal Elegy," *Studies in Philology* 51 (1954): 107–26, where the conventions in question, leading up to the consolation, are described.

worn gravity of "epitaph" with the pressing disorderliness of his particular sentiment. The opening, concealed list of commonplaces is an invocation, and the succeeding lines record a narrow, superb victory of tone.

Part of their somewhat mysterious success is embedded in the handling of rhythm: in the first stanza, all of the stressed syllables are rather heavily accented; the feet are slow though not ponderous. Yet degree of accent among the stressed syllables is kept distinct and varied: both of the trimeter lines more or less ascend from foot to foot in degree of accent, and both of the tetrameter lines contain slightly more pronounced accents in the second and fourth feet. This unusually severe pattern emphasizes the integrity of the line, and results in a slow but varying movement. Then, the second foot of the second stanza, where the poem begins a new direction, is by far the lightest foot so far. The pace is again quickened by a very light anapestic substitution in the third foot of the third line of this stanza, but with an effect difficult to describe that metrical detail releases into the slower rhythmical, syntactical, and tonal resolution of the last line.

The dignity of an imaginative tradition conflicts with the demands of a personal emotion; the force of that problem compelled the grace of "Rose Aylmer," a familiar little poem which has become a sort of Gioconda of eight-line poems. In wider terms, the problem is that of being deeply articulate, literate, and conscious — yet deeply skeptical of the value of those same qualities. In Landor, the tradition of the commonplace appears as a persistent state of mind, a sort of self-witnessing on the part of the intelligence. The difficulty of penetrating that which is given — including one's own resources — becomes a second subject in poem after poem.

When unwitting or irrelevant, a poem's tendency to gloomily witness its own processes may be boring or distracting. But Landor's melancholy strain of skepticism is usually quite conscious and controlled. In particular, some of the best poems express a qualified skepticism about the possibility of truly recalling the personal or historical past. The tone is melancholy because the poet's desire is not merely recall, but "consecration."

In Rossetti, and in Dowson and Lionel Johnson, the same quality sometimes appears as nostalgia: a wistful, wavering commitment to the past as a source of techniques and subjects. In fact, rather than distinguish the two directions of Landor's work as Romantic and Classic, it might be more accurate to speak of tendencies which recall the 'Nineties and of other tendencies which recall the English Renaissance. Certainly "Rose Aylmer" combines the indulgence of the one ("A night of memories and of sighs"— Dowson's delight!) with the painless, Jonsonian compression of the other. As the early Yeats and Pound are on one border of the mistland, much of Landor is a similar distance from the other frontier: hence the similarity between some of Landor and their early poems. The resemblance is plainest in poems on the immemorial themes of art and song, of "minstrelsy" — poetry, like "Rose Aylmer," of the apparently naïve sentiment.

Poems Treating
Commonplaces of Romantic Feeling

An awareness of speaking poetically within a literary tradition also pervades the poems which suggest this heading. If I have in part been describing a "poetry about poetry," it should be said that the relevant definition of poetry is a very large one; Landor's poems tend to be in some measure about the making, generalizing, particularizing qualities of the mind. The way in which this concern gives amplitude to a subject is exemplified by the "Fiesolan Idyl." In this poem Landor presents a Romantic subject, and his own Romantic sensibility; without being diminished, these are informed by an ironic self-consciousness, an awareness that there are other kinds of sensibility. This awareness lends a complexity which is not "metaphysical" but emotional and tonal.

The poem may be described as having three sources of energy: Landor the English poet living in an Italian villa; flowers, particularly the blossoms of a very tall orange tree; and an Italian peasant girl. Of the three, the flowers most consistently pervade the poem's sixty-two lines. These flowers are notable because they are treated, finally, purely as flowers — although, in the course of the poem, they are very insistently personified flowers indeed. The blossoms speak, whisper, point, reproach, become part of the girl, and the girl even becomes part of them. Nevertheless, this process is a brilliant piece of deliberate rhetoric, concluding as they emerge triumphantly as mere blossoms. Few other poets of Landor's time would treat flowers as "just flowers," symbolizing not even "nature," and no pre-Romantic would bother, unless writing a georgic. But Landor is a Romantic poet, and to bring the blossoms back to their identity as plants was for him an act of self-definition.

The poem is in plot and atmosphere a sexual encounter for which the orange tree provides a metaphor and an occasion. The season, the languid day, and the pervasively sensual tone are at once established in a series of elegantly restless and playful figures:

1 *Here, where precipitate Spring with one light bound*
2 *Into hot Summer's lusty arms expires;*
3 *And where go forth at morn, at eve, at night,*
4 *Soft airs, that want the lute to play with them,*
5 *And softer sighs, that know not what they want;*
6 *Under a wall, beneath an orange-tree*
7 *Whose tallest flowers could tell the lowlier ones*
8 *Of sights in Fiesole right up above,*
9 *While I was gazing a few paces off*
10 *At what they seemed to show me with their nods,*
11 *Their frequent whispers and their pointing shoots,*
12 *A gentle maid came down the garden-steps*
13 *And gathered the pure treasures in her lap.*

The lush, slow rhythm in an extended pulse of caesuras "at morn, at eve, at night, / Soft airs," is succeeded by the successful metrical device of repeating the caesura after the second foot in lines 5, 6, and (slightly) 7.[7] These are devices of artful over-extension, of tension nearly too prolonged. They are paralleled by the careless, plentiful chain of pretty descriptive personifications, and by the almost slackly delayed grammar. All of these effects end, as does the description of Landor's own condition, with the eleventh line; the girl is described in two lines un-adorned in diction, simple in grammar and syntax. These cool lines in fact narrate an event which the "I" of the opening does not see:

> 14 *I heard the branches rustle, and stept forth*
> 15 *To drive the ox away, or mule, or goat,*
> 16 *Such I believed it must be. How could I*
> 17 *Let beast o'er power them?*

The gentle, slightly comic, but intense situation is now pre-pared: the calmly attractive girl who will later be confused with the blossoms is mistaken for an animal. The poet who has shown that he can describe nature well, but in self-conscious, fla-grantly literary language, next explains that he would stand in a rainstorm to protect a flower; he explains this affection, first, by stating that flowers stimulate his memory and his imagina-tion. But with a shade of self-directed irony, already hinted by the enjambed "I" of line 16 above, Landor's affection for flowers, and his humanization of them, are restated. And now the justification is not their usefulness to the poet's mental life; flowers are to be saved for their own, more-than-botanical life:

> 25 *And 'tis and ever was my wish and way*
> 26 *To let all flowers live freely, and all die,*

7. See the first conversation of "Southey and Landor" (*Works*, 5:269):
Southey. . . . I agree with you that, in blank verse, the pause after the fourth syllable, which Pope and Johnson seemed to like best, is very tiresome if often repeated; and Milton seldom falls into it. But he knew where to employ it with effect: for example, in this sharp reproof, twice over. Verses 145 and 146.

> *Was she thy God, that her thou didst obey*
> *Before his voice?*

27 *Whene'er their Genius bids their soul depart,*
28 *Among their kindred in their native place.*

This extravagance is not an unblinking example of the so-called pathetic fallacy; rather, it is a complexly defined and conscious admission and evaluation of that "fallacy." The lines and the situation constitute a comic judgment of an attitude which, Landor admits, is an acquired, literary, and rather silly sophistication; the girl, genuinely simple and in innocent good sense, picks the flowers. She would no more indulge in Landor's poetical attitude than would an ox, a mule, or a goat, and she is therefore closer to the flowers than the man whose language fixes, praises, and metaphor-izes them. In a moment, he will help her pick them, violating his professed code.

The poem thus comprehends the melancholy distance which the poet's felt Romanticism creates between himself and the admired object — girl, flowers, late spring day; to realize this distance is not a denial of the Romantic feeling but part of its definition. The unfulfilled, suspended sexual relationship, with its brief rise of pitch at the end of the poem, embodies the sad distance between the mode of consciousness and the unconscious object which it would wed.

This is Romantic irony, but in the lightness of its wit (after which paraphrase lumbers) it is less postured, less self-inflated than Laforguian or Byronic Romantic irony; more judgment of the poet's own feeling is finally attained. At the same time, neither the feeling nor its intensity is disavowed. How could the above extravagance be followed? By a lovely, witty, plainer extravagance, by a five word sentence:

29 *I never pluck the rose; the violet's head*
30 *Hath shaken with my breath upon its bank*
31 *And not reproacht me; the ever-sacred cup*
32 *Of the pure lily hath between my hands*
33 *Felt safe, unsoil'd, nor lost one grain of gold.*

This arch little song ends with a quick, graceful transition to the girl picking blossoms, and the encounter; these in turn begin with an ambiguous moment in which the girl is merged with the sunlight and foliage:

> 34 *I saw the light that made the glossy leaves*
> 35 *More glossy; the fair arm, the fairer cheek*
> 36 *Warmed by the eye intent on its pursuit;*
> 37 *I saw the foot, that, altho half-erect*
> 38 *From its grey slipper, could not lift her up*
> 39 *To what she wanted: I held down a branch. . . .*

Sunlight, leaves, warm flesh combine in a single sensual experience. The sexuality, an earthier but no less delicate version of the opening metaphor, provides a comic social explanation for the sudden abandonment of religious respect for flowers: the girl has replaced them as the most arousing object of desirable, natural beauty. The next line gives an explicit explanation: "their hour / was come." Both of these reasons for profaning these flowers merely contribute to the powerfully implied explanation which is bodied forth in lines 41–47: by joining the girl, he has become able, briefly, to see the orange blossoms as orange blossoms, as she does.

We see the flowers now in the apotheosis of being merely what they are, and the poet sees them most vividly now, here, when they are not personified but lovingly, lingeringly displayed in precise, nearly botanical detail:

> 40 *And gather'd her some blossoms, since their hour*
> 41 *Was come, and bees had wounded them, and flies*
> 42 *Of harder wing were working their way thro*
> 43 *And scattering them in fragments underfoot.*
> 44 *So crisp were some, they rattled unevolved,*
> 45 *Others, ere broken off, fell into shells,*
> 46 *Unbending, brittle, lucid, white like snow,*
> 47 *And like snow not seen thro, by eye or sun:*

The insects emphasize that the bold "I never pluck the rose" presents an attitude toward "nature" which is opposite to nature itself: an attitude human and intellectual. But further, like the decay, the bees and flies comprise part of the atmosphere: tentative, "half-erect," yet somewhat overblown, and in some measure corrupt. Tone plays against tone, innocence against sophistication, ripeness against freshness, sensuality against lethargy, and sentimentality against its own wry, alert self-consciousness. The diction of this descriptive passage itself gains part of its effect by juxtaposing the latinate with the native: "scattering" with "fragments," "unevolved" with "crisp" and "rattled," "lucid" with "brittle." This intricate combining of tones, and the climate of near-fruition, are most explicit in the poem's conclusion. But, first, I should like to say something about metrical art throughout, as exemplified in the passages just quoted.

The pentameter is varied by a very flexible use of caesura and enjambment; and, within a grid of iambic feet (very infrequently replaced by a trochee, usually in the conservative first and third positions, or by a very light anapest), the degree of accent, among stressed syllables and among unstressed syllables, is greatly modulated. Thus, the *stressed* syllable in the fairly light third foot of line 37 receives *less* accent than the *unstressed* syllable "grey" in the next line. "Grey slipper" slows and concludes the rush over the line-ending which begins on the double pause ", that," in line 37. The resulting movement renders the foot and slipper more effective as description, and emphasizes them as metaphor. A similar, more marked, effect occurs in the preceding lines (35–36); here the movement is from the two caesuras, the first occurring in the middle of a foot, to the end of the more markedly accented, relatively pauseless, second line of the pair.

Opposite to the very light kind of iambic foot in the second position in line 35 are those in line 47, which ends the descriptive passage. We can describe this line — abstractly — as consisting of two iambs, a trochee, and two more iambs:

And like/snow not/seen thro,/by eye/or sun:

But the second iamb contains an unstressed syllable which is heavily accented, and the accented syllable of this foot is placed next to the even more accented first syllable of the trochee. So, in addition to the iambic norm, there is a trochaic movement, and a series of five syllables ascending in accent; the latter effects would be less subtle if the iambic norm were not maintained by Landor, or if one should neglect the norm utterly in reading. This line ends the description which is the fulcrum of the poem with a feeling of great effort for precision; the strained crescendo of the three feet analyzed spills into two distinct iambs which make the final, painstaking distinction of the description.

This matter is perhaps boring, and surely better heard than explained, but I dwell upon it because Landor's poem is dependent upon its rhythm, and this is especially true, if one can say such a thing, of the final resolution:

48 *Yet every one her gown received from me*
49 *Was fairer than the first . . . I thought not so,*
50 *But so she praised them to reward my care.*
51 *I said*: you find the largest.
                                    This indeed,
52 *Cried she*, is large and sweet.
                                    She held one forth,
53 *Whether for me to look at or to take*
54 *She knew not, nor did I; but taking it*
55 *Would best have solved (and this she felt) her doubt.*
56 *I dared not touch it; for it seemed a part*
57 *Of her own self; fresh, full, the most mature*
58 *Of blossoms, yet a blossom; with a touch*
59 *To fall, and yet unfallen.*
                                    She drew back
60 *The boon she tendered, and then, finding not*
61 *The ribbon at her waist to fix it in,*
62 *Dropt it, as loth to drop it, on the rest.*

These are the pleasures and sufferings of the Romantic whose relationship with experience consists of a tense, luxurious unconsummation: that subject is enclosed by a momentary encounter, in charming surroundings, between an unusually sensitive (see how his pains with syntax reflect his perception of the situation) intellectual and an Italian peasant girl. This is "estrangement," as the cliché goes; a familiar Romantic subject, based upon the dilemma that to be truly immersed in experience is to desire it no longer — conversely, consciously to desire immersion in unconscious nature is to be utterly distinct from it.

But Landor's poem is an idyll, a small and apparently casual incident: is it then simply an effete variation on a theme more fully handled by Keats and Shelley? I think that the intensity of the writing, and Landor's slow, careful definition of particular feelings, prevent the poem from being merely arch. And on the other hand, the modesty of the actual experience permits a variable lightness of tone; this element, used mostly for a sort of wistful self-deflation, increases rather than "lightens" the poem's emotional import. The evidence and final emergence of this import is in the writing of the poem's conclusion, in which the idea of an "idyll" attains great and subtle force as a human problem.

The encounter's conclusion completes the basic, ironic contrast between Landor's unnatural, restless piety toward "the natural" and the innocent, graceful barbarism of the girl — who is presented as an intrinsic part of "the natural." Her pleasure proceeds obviously from moment to moment, and she gathers blossoms in a spirit similar to that of the bees; for the poet, nearly-having is the boundary and definition of delight. The sexual and social version of this situation is not paramount; rather, it is the final and most explicit representation of the whole. Lines 48–50 introduce this social representation and its atmosphere, one in which an underlying complexity of feeling — mostly Landor's — struggles to maintain a surface of graceful simplicity — mostly hers. The long sequence of descriptive qualifications, modifying "every one was fairer than the first," emphasizes formally the difficulty of grasping the experience, in retrospect and at the moment.

This all but excessive subtlety of qualification is in one way relieved by the short, extremely simple dialogue. But the dialogue achieves that dignified simplicity through a method which affirms the impenetrability of experience. It has been said that Landor's poems sometimes read as though they were translations; here, the chaste and artificial simplicity of two italicized statements are translations, fictionally, of the more earthy simplicity of idiomatic Italian. The resultant language (Hemingway's mock-Spanish is a similar device) nicely solves a stylistic problem, preserving the scene's dreamlike remoteness as well as its intimate, earthbound, and pastoral qualities. But aside from this stylistic function, the two lines in their context exemplify the nature of this particular moment in the poem, and of other moments at which speech "resembles translation." The tentative and ambiguous atmosphere surrounding their conversation produces a consciousness that all language is after all a version of something. Thus, the effect is not cold, but tentative; not remote, but concerned with remoteness.

This moment is despite its delicacy a moment of severe — although perhaps delicious — separation. The division of the two people does not change, nor do their roles in it, but this time it is the girl who by praising them exaggerates the orange-flowers, with motives more direct and courteous, less complex and personal, than those which the poet had. Both people are eager to maintain a gracious delight in the day, the treeful of blossoms, their sexily flirtatious meeting.

The sentence after the dialogue suggests, formally as well as literally, the difficulty of their endeavor to prolong or ripen a mood. That suggestion would have less force if, for example, the pronouns of line 54 were returned to their more expected sequence,

I knew not, nor did she.

Avenues of concern are here expressed syntactically; the interpretation of the forever ambiguous gesture hovers first with her, the actor, and then with him, the witness. Similarly, in the runover from 54 to 55,

but taking it
Would best have solved, and this she felt, her doubt

and through the succeeding lines, in which the poet chooses the tense pleasures of not-having, avenues of concern are expressed by the frequent, hesitating stroke of the enjambment.

"Taking it" would "best solve" the situation. But "taking

it" (as opposed to the brief, irrevocable pleasure taken as a particular blossom falls gently and unaccepted to the pile) would disturb, through a small fruition, the suspended resolution of desire represented by the actions of "not-finding" and "drawing back" (lines 59 and 60). The impatience hinted at earlier in the poem has gone like a summer morning's haze, but the achievement of this idyllic clarity can come, for the sensibility of this poem, only through a kind of psychic abstention. That is to say, for the man defined in the poem, the idyll, the flawless pastoral mood, fulfills itself emotionally only when partial and arrested in fact. The greater part of the experience, all but a vital edge, must remain submerged in the imagination. Melancholy loss, associated with a certain kind of pleasure, is the inescapable lot of one who is acutely conscious of that pleasure.

In accord with this principle of having and not having, Landor, changing places with the girl, sees the flower "truly," though only to be able to say that it *seems like* something else. The poem, with the flowers, proceeds (roughly speaking) from metaphor, to sheer descriptive detail, to simile. The pathetic fallacy is not abandoned but articulated by the poet; and this fealty to a way of seeing which is his, and not hers, makes the sad, deprived quality of the closing image his also.

This is a poetry of sensibility and not of the "metaphysics" which Landor so detests;[8] the poems exemplify this frequently declared detestation in their sometimes almost imagistic pessimism about one's power to abstract the slightest generality from experience. A feeling and its motivation are carefully de-

8. Douglas Bush speaks of "his [Landor's] abhorrence of things metaphysical and his inability to understand things religious," but Bush's footnote on this remark walks into a joke by pagan Landor. Bush, perhaps momentarily more Christian than Humanist, fails to note the irony which Landor exerts "through the mouth of Porson," a friend whose learned, tipsy unruliness Landor found richly comic. Bush's note:

> One brief item may be quoted. After an explosive attack, through the mouth of Porson, on the "conventicle" allusions in the first version of *Laodamia*, the speaker avows that he is "not insensible to the

fined, and only by this definition are they generalized. Such a procedure seems merely modest only if we are accustomed to valuing poems according to how much one can devise to say about them; Landor wrote no "fragments" designed as inexhaustible stimulants to discussion for poetic nineteenth-century souls, or for twentieth-century scholarly ones. Rather, his poems are designed to leave nothing more to say, and his ideal of "clarity" indicates, beyond simple intelligibility, a stylistic utterness in the presentation of emotion.

To appreciate the magnitude and the ambition of a poem like "The Fiesolan Idyl" it is necessary to consider the difficulty of the stylistic jobs which are undertaken. For example, one may say that the orange-flowers proceed from metaphor to simile, but that is a crude approximation of the degree to which the flowers move, at any given moment, along a scale from nominal object to explicit analogy; if the comparison in lines 56–59 were more baldly analogical, the tone would be broken by the verb "fall" and by the picture of an upended girl. At the same time, the comparison is, to its just degree, made.

It is also worth pointing out that in the course of paraphrasing the poem it is impossible to avoid directing a sort of spiritual snobbery at the peasant girl; while the poem, with its shrewd awareness of the actual and by means of self-directed irony, avoids this patronizing attitude completely: so far as we know about what she thinks, the woman stands for an admirable simplicity. And this is true even though she becomes, at times, an object. Such accomplishments in controlling timbre and color constitute Landor's definition of a peculiar, nameless, and significant state of mind; the process is embedded throughout the writing. Self-aware identification of "Romantic" sentiments

warmly chaste morality which is the soul of it, nor indifferent to the benefits that literature on many occasions has derived from Christianity" (*Works*, V, 163). The last phrase is unconsciously illuminating.
I think that Bush's own remarks reveal *his* prejudices. Douglas Bush, *Mythology and the Romantic Tradition in English Poetry* (Cambridge, Mass.: Harvard University Press, 1937), p. 234, n. 7.

is, no less than the generation of a philosophy from such sentiments, a valid way of undertaking the most serious writerly ambitions.

Poems Treating Situations from Classical Myth or History

In "The Fiesolan Idyl," then, Landor portrays emotion which is to some extent beyond grasp, frustrated in relation to its own nature: the desire for a relaxed simplicity is itself complex and intense. The next rough category indicates his frequent concern with emotions which are lost, changed, or impenetrable in relation to time. Most obviously within this category are the *Hellenics* and, less interesting, the Greek and Roman dramatic scenes.

After attempting to summarize those of Landor's interests which underlie the *Hellenics*, I should like for a few pages to quote from a number of these poems to suggest the special tone of the whole group. Then, by a closer examination of "Dryope," a representative poem from the *Hellenics*, I hope to give a full example of Landor's imagination at work with mythological material. A true portrait of the *Hellenics*, and their splendor, will help show why *Chrysaor* is so bad, and why it has sometimes been considered Landor's greatest poem.

Many of the poems grouped together as *Hellenics* are in fact translations from Landor's own Latin. Another fact to be mentioned is Landor's distaste, affirmed in many prose statements, for "metaphysics" in poetry. And, in "The Fiesolan Idyl" and elsewhere, there is a distinct pessimism or reluctance in regard to the mind's relation to sensory experience. We thus have a writer who is pessimistic about his power to generalize perceptions and emphatically distrustful of speculative thought. He is faithful to old forms, to old myth, and even, in the original versions of these poems, to an old tongue. He depends upon his peculiar capacities of style, for originality; and upon the precise delineation of passion, for subject.

This slightly exaggerated portrait serves to distinguish Landor's position clearly from the often discursive Renaissance methods which it in other ways resembles. Landor worked within all but constricting bounds, and an understanding of these will dispel much of the cliché in Landor criticism. The familiar "chisel" and "marble" connote the coldness of stone and metal as well as the polished hardness, but coldness is quite exactly the wrong word. Poems in which the intellectual treatment of feeling is more stylistic than conceptually explicit tend to require, in the pursuit of weight and import, great intensity of passion. Accordingly, one's most recurrent criticism of Landor's poems is not that a poem is wanting in feeling, but that it insists upon too much feeling. As with the other Romantic poets, the shouting is at moments inadequately or obscurely justified.

Landor's "coldness" can often be better described, then, as extravagance. This is the case with most of the hyperbolically ardent political poems. Even the many poems expressing friendship or admiration are either gracefully or embarrassingly hyperbolic, and it is probably fair to generalize that Landor is at his best when dealing with powerfully sensuous experience or with the classic Great Passions of death, love, and hate. He was prevented from even venturing some "philosophical" subjects — not only by a Romantic aversion toward abstraction, but also by a personal refusal to generate the mere impression of complexity by means of a Shelley-like vagueness. Such restricting habits of procedure limit most of Landor's poems of republican feeling to fustian or sloppy assertion.

In other instances, supposed "coldness" may be the reader's misconception of Landor's peculiar, in a way sentimental, variety of stoicism, one in which restraint or distance transforms, without reducing, emotion. A few exclamatory declarations of passion for the peasant girl, and of rapture toward the pretty flowers, would reduce "The Fiesolan Idyl" to cold ash; in the most valuable of Landor's work, the universal passions which are his material are very specially qualified. One aspect of this qualification, that peculiar stoicism founded upon the grace of art, is common to several brilliant poems within the *Hellenics*.

Landor turned to myth because he knew it, but also because myth provided, not so much the source, but the setting for a certain kind of incident; and incident, rather than reflective abstraction, provides his most congenial material. The *Hellenics*, we can generalize, are poems which treat the violent, the sensuous, or the otherwise passionate as hidden, isolated in the expanding swarm of time. Or, more simply, they deal with myth as itself, but within a framing, sensitive awareness of the myth's remoteness from the teller. The question of whether the myth can ever be known immediately and as itself shadows these poems, and this overtone clearly resembles the frustrated longing toward nature examined in the preceding section. Nature and history, in their common quality of elusive apartness, have similar and often simultaneous roles in Landor's work; in the poem beginning "Ye who have toil'd," the past and the nonhuman "natural" merge into a single, painfully haunting Other.

But Landor's concern with the myth itself is not the same as a dedication to recreating old story in its true lineaments. Landor held no such scholarly ambition — no more than Wordsworth desired to record folk dialects of Westmorland. Rather, Landor's treatment of "sources" was cavalier in the sense that he did not care about "fidelity" at all. The vital matter for the poet is the impression of authenticity, the fictive illusion that the satyr, or the leech-gatherer, is actual. Landor's Pound-like attitude in this matter is directly indicated by some remarks on translation contained in a letter written shortly after he completed the first translation of the *Idyllia Heroica*. Landor paraphrased a "most wise and philosophical remark of Novalis":

> A translation is either grammatical, or periphrastic, or mythic. Mythical translations are translations in the highest style: they present the pure, essential, perfect character of the individual

work of art. They do not give us the actual work, but its ideal. *As yet I believe there exists no complete model in this kind. It requires a head thoroughly imbued with both the poetical and the philosophical spirit, in their entire plenitude.*[9]

And, when writing mythological poetry, as when translating, one proceeds after the spirit of the thing, doubtful of "complete" success. One strives in the way of the myth makers and remakers of antiquity, and recreates freely in order to make the matter moving and immediate at the same time that it is imposing, remote and marvelous. The tension between these qualities — what is remote and what is moving — is especially Landor's.

The sense of actuality depends upon the most immediately striking quality of the *Hellenics*: the sensory details are of a very rich and persuasive liveliness. This is even true, perhaps most true, of the more conventional elements. These pastoral meadows have real grass, and the hair curling down onto Pan's hoof has weight and texture. Probably the earliest pure example of this characteristic Landorian technique is the second line (first version; the line was removed, but salvaged in a later poem) of *Gebir*:

> *When old Silenus call'd the Satyrs home,*
> *Satyrs then tender-hooft and ruddy-horn'd, . . .*

The satyrs smell of the pinewoods, not the lamp. We are told that they are young neither directly nor by means of a "spiritual" quality like innocence, friskiness, blitheness; the creatures are young by detail, the descriptive means of the hunt, the farm, or, nearly, of the zoology classroom. (Characteristically, the two vivifying details, in conjunction with the word "then," emphasize at one time the immediate reality and the great distance in time of the scene described.)

Yet, fleshed with life as they are, the characters in these poems are heightened and mythological. Although humanly fallible

9. R. H. Super, *Walter Savage Landor: A Biography* (New York: New York University Press, 1954), p. 377.

and passionate they are the products of selective, shrewd exaggeration; their experience of bruises, pinpricks, and kisses, as well as of spells and murders, is somewhat beyond the human. This effect is sometimes a product of the intense realization of the tiny image, a preternatural, Herrick-like concentration of the observing senses:

> *He may snatch off my slipper while I kneel*
> *To Pan, upon the stone so worn aslant*
> *That it is difficult to kneel upon*
> *Without my leaving half a slipper loose.*
> *"Lysander, Alcanor and Phanŏe," lines 20–23*

Or, the mythic overtone may be a deft, slight element of exaggeration — the exaggeration of the caricature at least as often as that of the heroic; Pan has been blinded by a quill-point, and medicinal flowers are pressed on the wounds:

> *But when they toucht his eyes he stampt and yell'd*
> *And laid wide-open his sharp teeth until*
> *The quivering nostril felt the upper lip.*
> *"Cupid and Pan," second version, lines 100–103*

Both of these poems also exemplify the frequency of convincing erotic incident in the *Hellenics*. The passage above continues as Phanŏe talks about Alcanor; long, it is worth quoting for the rich, gradual development:

> *Little cares he for Pan: he scarcely fears*
> *That other, powerfuller and terribler,*
> *To whom more crowns are offered than to Zeus,*
> *Or any God beside, and oftener changed.*
> *In spring we garland him with pointed flowers,*
> *Anemone and crocus and jonquil,*
> *And tender hyacinth in clustering curls;*
> *Then with sweet-breathing mountain strawberry;*
> *Then pear and apple blossom, promising*
> *(If he is good) to bring the fruit full-ripe,*
> *Hanging it round about his brow, his nose,*
> *Down even to his lips. When autumn comes,*
> *His russet vine-wreath crackles under grapes:*
> *Some trim his neck with barley, wheat, and oat;*
> *Some twine his naked waist with them: and last*

> *His reverend head is seen and worshipt through*
> *Stiff narrow olive-leaves, that last till spring.*
> *Say, ought I not to fear so wild a boy,*
> *Who fears not even* him! *but once has tried*
> *By force to make me pat him, after prayers?*
> *How fierce then lookt the God! And from above*
> *How the club reddened, as athirst for blood!*
> *Yet fearing and suspecting the audacious,*
> *Up Maenalos I must, for there my herd*
> *Is browsing on the thorn and citisus*
> *At random.*
> > "*Lysander, Alcanor and Phanŏe*," lines 24–29

And the wrestling of Cupid and Pan develops into the main plot element of "Cupid and Pan": a casual and sprightly homosexuality perhaps shocking to the modern and un-Hellenic orthodoxy which demands a more solemn, apocalyptic or respectful tone for the subject:

> > *and then advanced,*
> *Trembling to intertwine his hairy shank*
> *With that soft thigh and trip him up, nor ceast*
> *To press the yielding marble from above.*
> *He grew less anxious to conclude the fight*
> *Or win it; but false glory urged him on.*
> *Cupid, now faint and desperate, seized one horn;*
> *Pan swung him up aloft; but artifice*
> *Fail'd not the boy; nay, where the Arcad cried*
> Conquered *at last, and ran both hands about*
> *The dainty limbs, pluckt out from the left wing*
> *Its stiffest feather, and smote both his eyes.*
> > *second version, lines 48–59*

In fact, Douglas Bush's remark that "Landor's mature manner is more Hellenistic and Ovidian than Hellenic"[10] is certainly apt at least in this: few English poets have written as often, as lovingly, and as effectively about sexual pleasure. He is very different from his contemporaries in his ability to present sexuality uncluttered with ambiguity or philosophy; a measure of how different some of these contemporaries could be from Landor is in De Quincey's series on Landor in *Tait's*

10. Bush, *Mythology and the Romantic Tradition*, p. 241.

Edinburgh Magazine.[11] De Quincey clearly considers Landor a very great poet, but he regrets the "coarseness" which he believes Landor to have contracted as the sad result of living for too long amid Italians. The examples of this coarseness are the indecorous words "bosom" and "thigh"; De Quincey explains that uncorrupted, unlatinized Englishmen are willing to use these words in their proper situations — referring, say, to parts of animals or fowl — but not as Landor does, with reference to ladies. De Quincey is bantering, but not kidding. Landor surpasses his time, a time which regretted Herrick's "blemishes," in achieving the spirit associated with Marlowe and with Landor's hero Ovid. Like theirs, his verse is erotic but the opposite of coarse:

> *To play at love, she knew,*
> *Stopping its breathings when it breathes most soft,*
> *Is sweeter than to play on any pipe.*
> *She play'd on his: she fed upon his sighs:*
> *They pleased her when they gently waved her hair,*
> *Cooling the pulses of her purple veins,*
> *And when her absence brought them out they pleased.*
> *"The Hamadryad," lines 206–12*

Landor's use of erotic incident is delicate, just as his use of physical violence is restrained in tone, no matter how extreme the actual events.

Furthermore, the sensuous atmosphere of the *Hellenics* is extended to all of nature, so that every physical description becomes to a degree voluptuous. Quite often, with or without the catalyst of myth, nature is treated with a witty sensuality. Here is Apollo, the Sun:

> *With light he irrigates*
> *The earth beneath, to all things gives their hue,*
> *Motion, and graceful form, and harmony:*
> *But now the tresses of his golden hair*
> *Wills he to fall and his warm breath to breathe*
> *On Dryope alone; her he pursues*
> *Among the willow of pubescent flower*
> *And fragrant bark stript off the tender twigs,*

11. "Notes on W. S. Landor," *Tait's Edinburgh Magazine*, 14(1847):99.

> *Moist, split, and ready for the basket-braid.*
> *He followed her along the river-bank,*
> *Along the shallow where the Nereids meet*
> *The Dryads.*
>> *"Dryope," second version, lines 6–17*

This vivid reincarnation is the goal, if not always the accomplishment, of all neoclassic art which treats such material; Landor's model, the Syracusan Theokritos, made a reputation by showing simple, idyllic grace among authentic sheep and foliage, and Ovid told worn-out stories in a new way that was based, for all of its artfulness, upon the senses. But the other striking aspect of the *Hellenics,* served by the element of sensuality, is uniquely Landor's: these incidents of great sensory immediacy are framed within a continuing theme of distance. The poems often advocate a detachment which is to come from our realization that time is enormous, and crowded with past and forgotten passions. The effect is in a measure sentimental, which is to say that the remoteness is used to make the passion more poignant, just as the intensity of the passion is a measure of time's enveloping hugeness. "Even *this,*" the poem asserts, "has become remote." One of the boldest presentations of this motif is in the rather melodramatic poem "Drimacos," which unfolds a situation of death, rebellion, and self-sacrifice involving Drimacos and his foster son Eiarinos. The poem begins like several of the *Hellenics* with a recitation of reigns, emphasizing historical remoteness, and with an even more explicit announcement of "dark ages":

> *In Crete reign'd Zeus and Minos; and there sprang*
> *From rocky Chios (but more years between)*
> *Homer. Ah! who near Homer's side shall stand?*
> *A slave, a slave shall stand near Homer's side.*
> *Come from dark ages forth, come, Drimacos!*

And the 136 line poem ends:

> *Nor Muse, nor Memory her mother, knows*
> *The sequel: but upon the highest peak*
> *Of Chios is an altar of square stone*

> *Roughened by time, and some believe they trace*
> *In ancient letters, cubit-long, the words*
> Drimacos *and* Eiarinos *and* Zeus.

This passage concludes a poem which constitutes a sort of
lyric revelation of what is a potential heroic plot; as so often
when reading Landor, we are almost led to suspect that some-
where there is a verse romance upon which the poem is based.
"Icarios and Erigone" treats a simpler, more credible (and
more violent) incident; the poem thus further exemplifies the
several kinds of situation included within the one general, and
at first incongruous seeming, tone of the *Hellenics.*

The idea of pre-Hellenic and pre-Athenian Greece fascinated
Landor; the action of "Icarios and Erigone" takes place, we are
told at once, in almost prehistoric Greece:

> *Ere Pallas in compassion was their guide*
> *They never stowed away the fruits of earth*
> *For winter use; nor knew they how to press*
> *Olive or grape:*
> > *lines 5–8*

Icarios, however, has made wine, the first seen there. Erigone
is his daughter. Her suitors come to a feast, and perhaps a third
of the hundred and twenty-odd lines richly describe a classic
peasant opulence: "The milk, / buzzing in froth beneath un-
steady goat" (lines 12–13), "The steam hung on the rafters,
where were nail'd / Bushes of savory herbs, and figs and dates"
(lines 50–51); finally, the host proudly brings the grapes which
he alone then fermented. The description is very full, almost
perversely so:

> *he now*
> *Descended, holding in both arms a cask,*
> *Fictive, capacious, bulging: cork-tree bark*
> *Secured the treasure: wax above the mouth,*
> *And pitch above the wax. The pitch he brake,*
> *The wax he scraped away, and laid them by,*
> *Wrenching up carefully the cork-tree bark.*
> *A hum was heard. "What! are there bees within?"*
> *Euphorbas cried. "They came then with the grapes,"*

> *Replied the elder, and pour'd out clear juice*
> *Fragrant as flowers, and wrinkled husks anon.*
> *"The ghosts of grapes!" cried Phanor. . . .*
>
> *lines 60–71*

This exclamation, marked as a bad omen, occurs after the poem has run half of its length. Rapidly, in forty lines, the suitors drink, swear friendship, quarrel roughly over Erigone, and then turn angrily upon Icarios; the climax is, in contrast with the descriptions, abrupt and understated. Erigone starts to run out, after the men, for help:

> *Before her sprang*
> *Moera, and howl'd and barkt, and then return'd*
> *Presaging. They had dragg'd the old man out*
> *And murdered him.*
>
> *lines 105–8*

Line 111 pictures the dog and the corpse's "unclosed" eyes, "rais'd toward the stars of heaven." Then comes a double space and the seventeen lines which, though an epilogue, yet contain what seemingly ought to have been treated as the main incident: the destruction of one another by the rioters.

> *Raise thine [eyes], for thou hast heard enough, raise thine*
> *And view Bootes bright among those stars,*
> *Brighter the Virgin: Moera too shines there.*
> *But where were the Eumenides? Repress*
> *Thy anger. If the clear calm stars above*
> *Appease it not, and blood must flow for blood,*
> *Listen, and hear the sequel of the tale.*
>
> *lines 113–19*

But despite that last line, the poem is not narrative; we have an allegorical descriptive passage next which precedes and pre-empts the one-line summary of events, a summary still postponed for the last moment.

> *Wide-seeing Zeus looked down; as mortals knew*
> *By the woods bending under his dark eye,*
> *And huge towers shuddering on the mountain tops,*
> *And stillness in the valley. . . .*
>
> *lines 120–23*

Jove is deduced rather than unequivocally seen, and the idea of divine retribution capping a narrative is further diluted by his uncertain effectiveness; he lifts his arm "but struck them not." The poem concludes with another brief summary of violent action:

> *by each other's blow*
> *They fell; some suddenly; but more beneath*
> *The desperate gasp of long-enduring wounds.*
> *lines 126–28*

The poem is not narrative; neither is it dramatic in any sense, rather ignoring or glossing over the moments of psychological crisis for the characters. These characters are vividly realized as members of a single, memorably colored frieze, but as individuals they are generalized and their passions are assumed rather than defined. What then is the point of this lyric which tells us, just as the daughter finds her father's body — fine moment for a speech — "thou hast heard enough"?

The point is, partly, "Repress / Thy anger." The poem tells us that there were and presumably are such things as murder, passion, anger, and so forth, although only in a minimal, conventional way are these matters defined. The main statement is that of all idylls: "Icarios and Erigone" is another definition of the enormous, absolute interval separating the eternal and fictive (Moera in the "clear calm start above") from the actual and contingent. What happened, what the passion was, is incidental, part of "the ghost of wine"; the two important elements are, first, the irrefutable realization of the actual life, in a noisy room with smoke-polished beams, and, second, the equally irrefutable realization of the "clear calm stars." The nature of myth is to treat lust, hatred, and other anxious, timebound brutalities, while the myth's own time is vaguely boundless, rather a device. Daphne "becomes," but in a way always was, the laurel: this is mythology-making at its primary level. At a more sophisticated level, Landor considers the process and contemplates the primitive banquet and its relation to the constellations. He brings to the myth the slightly decadent, nineteenth-century stoicism of his short poems. This melancholy, perceptive detachment explains in part why Landor could refer to such poems as his "idylls."

This stoic "moral" is often quite explicit. "Pan and Pitys" begins:

> *Cease to complain of what the Gods decree,*
> *Whether by death or (harder!) by the hand*
> *Of one prefer'd thy loves be torne away,*
> *For even against the bourn of Arcady*
> *Beats the sad Styx, heaving its wave of tears,*
> *And nought on earth so high but care flies higher.*

And after a sensual scene in which Pan and Pitys appear as earthly creatures enjoying the woods, one another, and their homely spat, there is an abrupt disaster followed by a picture of the distraught but now mythological Pan. The theme of rapture and loss serves the larger theme of the irrevocable past. The poetry attempts to reembody myth as what it is, but also maintains a self-conscious awareness that this goal cannot be fulfilled perfectly, and that the attempt alters the subject which it touches. When the narrator of "The Marriage of Helena and Menelaos" speaks as one ignorant of future events (or when Iphigeneia in the scene "Shades of Agamemnon and Iphigeneia" speaks in ignorance of all that followed her death), Landor is following Ovid's *Heroides,* and the exercises of rhetoric-schools; but he is also conjoining the human and inhuman qualities of myth. Such formal devices enforce this subject no less than "realistic" touches like the young brat Theseus making swan-faces to tease Leda ("The Altar of Modesty," lines 12–24).

Many of the concerns so far mentioned are combined in "Dryope," a poem in which their actual poetic working may be illustrated in detail. The poem presents, in the full force of its implications for Landor, a divine seduction — the great mythological theme of the god who ravishes a human. The poem opens with one of Landor's characteristically successful latinisms of sentence, and with a reign-recital:

1 *Famous and over famous Oeta reign'd*
2 *Dryope: him beauteous Polydora bare*
3 *To the river-god Sperchios: but above*
4 *Mother and sire, far brighter in renown,*
5 *Was Dryope their daughter, the beloved*
6 *Of him who guides thro' heaven his golden car.*

The listing of names, which is made more prominent by the metrical and syntactical features of the first sentence, has a deliberate flavor of the archaic and the conventional; the end-stopped climax of this opening, and the epithet, prepare us for another conventional element: an enumeration of the god's attributes. It is vital to Landor's theme that Apollo, Delios, be enormously magnificent; this is Apollo in all of his attributes. He is, indeed, the sun:

7 *Showering his light o'er all things, he endues*
8 *All things with colour, grace and song gives he,*
9 *But never now on any condescends*
10 *To lower his shining locks; his roseate lips*
11 *Breathe an ambrosial sigh on none but her.*

He is the sun, color, song, life, everything; but the brilliant metaphor of line 10 conducts us from the god as a group of abstractions and a huge natural phenomenon to the god as a lover. This graceful transition emphasizes the distinction by skimming over it: that the nexus is metaphorical, anchored in the word "shining," establishes that the disparity is considerable. The poem assumes its conventions so artfully that such devices have their effect without being noticed.

This is also the case in the matter of tense. The repetition of "all things" at different points in lines 7 and 8; the series "showering," "endues," and "gives"; and the comma at the caesura in line 8, which seems for a moment to divide a series of nouns but in fact divides a series of clauses: all of these mark a little internal lyric enumerating Apollo's attributes with concealed repetition, and the "now" of line 9 seems to insert the theme of remoteness: gods no longer visit men. But this interpretation necessitates that in line 11 the present tense "Breathe" must signify a myth-time in which Orion constantly "hunts" and Philomela "complains." This suggestion does remain a part of the poem's rhetorical effect, but the succeeding lines show that the present tense in fact describes Dryope's actual pursuit by a fleshly Apollo in the historical time which precedes the poem's main incident. The lines leave little doubt of this fact if only because they are so scenically realized, with the twigs of willow stripped for basket-braid. I have already quoted (pp. 58–59) the passage from the 1859 *Hellenics*; the willows in the version being discussed are just as quotable:

> 12 *He follows that shy Nymph thro' pathless ways,*
> 13 *Among the willows in their soft grey flowers,*
> 14 *In their peeled boughs odorous, and amid*
> 15 *The baskets white and humid, incomplete. . . .*

Yet as this present-tense dumbshow closes we are reminded, by the presence of mythical beings, of the suggestion that his following of the Nymph takes place out of time:

> 18 *He follows where the Nereids watch their fords*
> 19 *While listen the Napaean maids around.*
> 20 *Tending one day her father's sheep she heard*
> 21 *A flute in the deep valley; then a pipe. . . .*

The introduction, largely by means of unobtrusive changes in tense, establishes Landor's interfusion of the sensual and the remote qualities of myth.

The past tense with which the flutenote is heard announces the immediate incident. "Dryads and Hamadryads" race toward Dryope, and one lightly chides her, incidentally praising the god whose flawless magnificence is to preside over the day, as over Landor's poem:

> 25 *Knowest thou not the day when all should sing*
> 26 Paean *and* Io Paean? *Shunnest thou*
> 27 *The lord of all, whom all the earth adores,*
> 28 *Giver of light and gladness, warmth and song?*
> 29 *And willest thou that Dryope stands above*
> 30 *Admetos? from thy sight thus banishing*

31 *And shutting from thy fold the son of Jove."*
32 *She, proud and joyous at the gay reproof,*
33 *Stood silent. They began the dance and games.*

He is glory, and she is glorious through him. The maidens sing
the hymn to Delios, and near Dryope "a lyre shone out," the
first of the god's forms; she does not know where it came from,
but begins to play the "glimmering strings," looking at them
one by one, "knowingly,"

41 *and speaks*
42 *(As if it heard her) to it, now on lap*
43 *And now on bosom fondly laying it.*

Suddenly, the plectron turns to a snake. They scream and
scatter, but the supernatural event threatens the realistic atmosphere of the poem — which is at once reinstated by one of
Landor's obsessively minute, meticulous details, an image which
is also a sort of comic subplot version of Dryope's coming ravish-
ment:

47 *striving to rise,*
48 *Autonoë prest upon a fragile reed*
49 *Her flattened hand, nor felt it: when she saw*
50 *The blood, she suckt the starting globe, and sought*
51 *The place it sprang from.*

The full description of the "globe," with its pun on "starting"
and its other careful graces, establishes the tonal presence of
the idyll-teller while also establishing the physical truth of
the scene. This passage appears as the maidens panic, but one
soon turns her head, "Fearful til pity overcame her fear." She
cries out:

"Look back! Look back!
60 *See how that creature licks her lips, her eyes,*
61 *Her Bosom! How it seizes! How it binds*
62 *In the thick grass her struggles!*

. . . .

67 *Phoebus! come hither! aid us! Ah, what now*
68 *Would the beast do? how swells his horrid crest?"*

The god has been the instrument of earthly music and now as ravisher becomes the most earthly of creatures, a reptile. The speech, it should be noticed, is an appeal to "Apollo proud of Python slain." When it is interrupted by the poet's own voice, that voice uses the traditional superstitions which surround reptiles to echo subtly the original list of Apollo's attributes; this time the emphasis is upon the qualities shared with the chameleon, a beast which supposedly partakes of air. This emphasis is balanced by the comic transposition which brings the god serpent from the air to earth:

> 69 *Various and manifold the dragon brood.*
> 70 *Some urge their scales along the ground, and some*
> 71 *Their wings aloft, some yoked to fiery cars,*
> 72 *And some, tho' hard of body, melt in air.*

The lilt upon the last word of line 70, and the whole movement of the passage from its initial end-stop to the concluding one, enforce a light yet awed attitude toward godly and reptilian shape-shifting.

Intensity of experience, seen from the outside, is hard to conceive, and as the nymphs now on a hill above argue about what is happening below, at the scene of the shape-shifting, some are terrified, but one tries to pacify the others by in effect imagining the glory on a smaller scale. The suspended, restless sensuality of the passage recalls the "Fiesolan Idyl" and Landor's special way of seeing sensory experience:

> 80 *"Are there not many things that may deceive*
> 81 *The sight at first? might not a lizard seem*
> 82 *A dragon? and how pleasant in hot days*
> 83 *To hold a lizard to the breast, and tempt*
> 84 *Its harmless bitings with the finger's end. . . .*

The experience is small, languid, with an element of frustration. A contrasting image is that of the glory itself, after the watchers have noted how Dryope puts her hand on the creature's neck, how she "treats it like a sister," and, "far as we are off, / Lo! how it shines!" Delios emerges in a remarkable passage which is, somehow, abstractly visual:

93 *And now again the creature is transformed.*
94 *Lizard nor serpent now, nor tortoise-shell*
95 *Chelys, is that which purple flutters round,*
96 *And which is whiter here and darker there,*
97 *Like violets drifted o'er with shifting hail.*
98 *Golden the hair that fluctuates upon neck*
99 *None of its own. A bland ethereal glow*
100 *Ran over and ran thro' the calmer maid.*
101 *At last her fellow Nymphs came all around,*
102 *And Delios stood before them, manifest*
103 *No less to them than to his Dryope:*
104 *For with a radiant nod and arm outstretcht*
105 *He call'd them back; and they obey'd his call.*
106 *He lookt upon them, and with placid smile*
107 *Bespake them, drawing close his saffron vest.*

The god himself is pure, matterless color, an ecstasy of shade and motion; his manifestation to Dryope is vague, sexual, paradoxical. He becomes manlike for the audience with the Nymphs. They come near him with downcast eyes, knowing and fearing his enormous potency, some of the most noted examples of which ("When the woods crasht and perisht under him," "and Python graspt in death") are now recounted, repeating the god's-praise motif. The attitude of those who approach the Olympian splendor without the intimacy of Dryope, the chosen one, is summarized:

118 *Potent of good they knew him, and of ill,*
119 *And closed the secret in their prudent hearts.*

Such repetitions maintain the poem's lyric movement despite the seemingly narrative structure; with the completion of this passage, we have seen, as fully as may be shown, the god who descends to mate with sub-Olympian flesh. Attention now turns to the woman who has mated with a more-than-earthly magnificence. First there is a moment of contrast with the "prudent hearts" through whom we see, and whose limitations we of course share:

120 *At first they would have pitied the hard fate*
121 *Of Dryope; but when she answered not*

122 *The words of pity, in her face they lookt*
123 *Stealthily.*

The next paragraph, the peak of the poem, describes one who has been embraced by the intense light which these others fear:

123   *Soft the moisture of her brow,*
124 *Languid the luster of her eyes; a shame*
125 *Rosier and richer than before suffused*
126 *Her features, and her lips were tinged with flame*
127 *A god inspired, and worthy of that God.*

This passage is in form and effect another of Landor's disguised interior songs, used to mark and develop a crest in a poem's movement. By beginning the first sentence (and the paragraph) after three syllables of line 123, Landor introduces a line of the seven-syllable measure sometimes called beheaded tetrameter ("Queen and huntress, chaste and fair," "Soft the moisture of her brow"). This countermovement to the blank verse continues through the strong caesura after the fourth foot of line 124, but although this pseudo-line begins with a stressed syllable, it is a "line" of eight, not seven syllables, and so contributes toward the subsequent reassertion of pentameter in line 125. Of course, the feat, the aesthetic power, is that the pentameter has never disappeared; similarly, the tetrameter movement not only survives in the hint of a caesura after the fourth foot of line 125, but reappears in its seven-syllable form in the second half of line 126. All of this countermeasure would not be effective enough to be noticeable were it not for the further tightening effect of rhyming upon the metrically isolated word "shame." This word appears when the tetrameter element has most nearly mastered the blank verse; thus "flame," running-over into the final disappearance of the song measure in a very stable blank-verse line (127), knits the lines into a coherent strophe. The unobtrusive rhythmical art of the passage alters its literal statement a great deal, and in very complex ways; for example, the song-rhythm and the alliteration make the description more concentrated, more dance-like, more erotic, as well as more serious in timbre. Although it is impossible to trace the causal workings of this rhetoric, we can recognize that they are there, illustrating that for a master verse is not a tune to which prose is set, but a vital and intricate part of meaning.

In this case, the picture of Dryope's erotic afterglow acquires a formal quality, and in the context of Apollo's power and fluidity, which have been repeatedly celebrated, her oblivious and formalized rapture is an emblem of the absolute difference between those who have and have not coupled with a god. The wedding of the perfect and the earthbound was seen from a distance and imperfectly by the other nymphs. And, they cannot tell anyone else even what they saw, because

132   *they had lookt too near and seen too well,*
133 *And had invoked the God with dance and hymn;*
134 *Beside, Diana would have sore avenged*
135 *Her righteous brother, who deals openly*
136 *With mortals, and few facts from them conceals.*

Furthermore, this isolation of the event is increased in the final lines, not only as they show it passing further into Dryope's memory, but as Dryope herself passes into chronicle. The characteristic frame, the reminder of the present, is especially effective since its references to Dryope as wife, as mother, and as history follow so soon after her memorably sensuous embodiment:

137 *Dryope soon became Andraemon's wife,*
138 *And mother of Amphissos. Every spring*
139 *They chaunt her praises; hers, who trill'd so well*
140 *The plectron of Apollo; in the vale*
141 *Of her own shady Oeta do they sing.*

The most important thing to be said about this poem is that it is about a god, Apollo, who comes to earth and makes love with a mortal maiden. That is not to say that Landor fails to reinterpret myth; he reinterprets it as myth. The ideas traditionally associated with Apollo — light, warmth, physical beauty, song, poetry, power — are incorporated in a traditional theme — that of the divine lover. Landor uses Apollo as a means of representing in his poem a kind of brilliance, whose immutability is established by the praise which constitutes the poem's opening passage. The plot supplies a chosen mortal ravished by brilliance, and her mortality is established by her praise in the poem's closing passage. An intense, beautiful, and explicit sexuality changes the traditional incident of Olympian seduction without sacrificing its quality of mystery.

The traditional incident, is, in fact, permeated with the poet's Romantic anxiety. Apollo's shape-shifting; the difficulty of the nymphs in recognizing and then in approaching him; the remoteness of ecstatic Dryope from the nymphs; the contrast between the Sun and "Andraemon's wife": the emphasis upon all of these is an emphasis upon loss, upon the sad brevity or distance of the most powerful experience. Apollo "deals openly/With mortals, and few facts from them conceals." This statement is an ironic reference to the secrecy in which Apollo, source of light, will keep this seduction, but it is also an ironic reference to the uncompromised division between perfection and imperfection, in which his open dealing does us no good. The idea signified by Apollo, though awkward to paraphrase, is not complex or obscure; that is, the poem's mode is suitable, it does not attempt to embody metaphysics in character, and its representation of "positive, intense, uncomplicated experience" (to attempt a paraphrase) succeeds. Dryope's brief elevation is an emblem of simple ideational value and of emotional subtlety. A brilliant poem, "Dryope" is neither the best nor the worst of the *Hellenics*. Because of the large area of experience which the character Apollo is made to suggest in his attributes and metamorphoses, the poem may be called the most representative of the group.

Chrysaor: Treatment of Myth as Archetype Rather Than Commonplace

But "Dryope" is, after all, a poem about a god who seduces a mortal virgin. And our critics have found myth in so many places that we hardly know how to value it, or deal with it, in mythology. And from another direction Douglas Bush, with enormous prestige in the matter, says that "mythological poetry in which myths are merely retold is, if not dead, at least of a very inferior order." [12] The phrase "merely retold," like Bush's criterion that the poem should "carry modern implications," [13] is ambiguous, but Bush goes on to explain in his next sentence: "The author of *Chrysaor* had a message, the author of the *Hellenics* had none." [14] Bush says of *Chrysaor* that "probably no modern English poem of comparable power is less known to the generality of readers." [15] But *Chrysaor* is a poorly written and foolishly conceived poem of which it may be said that, more than anything else by Landor, it recalls Shelley. In Landor's case the bad poetry is not the result of ineptitude, but of an ambitious, systematic attempt at an epic style.

Now, I believe that the job for students of Landor's poetry is not to reform "our" estimate of Landor, for so far as such things can be determined in the absence of a poetic Stock Exchange, that estimate seems to me to be quite high. The job rather is to discover and implement ways of approaching and discussing Landor's work. He is on enough of the better syllabuses, probably, but although we value the poems we tend to forget why we value them, and so embalm them as "skillful." His methods are easy to mistake; in the case of mythological poetry, although he did not write the way classical writers did, he often, like them, retold myth in a way that was charged with his own interests through the inevitable means of style, and not through political or metaphysical allegory. Because Landor's mature procedure was unique in his time, we tend to misunderstand it. And so in this further section on mythology I should like to suggest that Bush's justly respected study of English mythological poetry treats Landor as though he were someone else. The evidence of this injustice is in the relative appraisal of *Chrysaor* and the *Hellenics*. I have explained why

12. Bush, *Mythology and the Romantic Tradition*, p. 244.
13. *Ibid.*
14. *Ibid.*
15. *Ibid.*, p. 238.

I think that the *Hellenics* are not completely described by Ernest de Selincourt, quoted approvingly by Bush: "it was Landor's achievement to bring into an age of romantic taste and sentiment, and of a growingly oppressive modernity, tortured with introspection and overburdened with its own problems, something of the peculiar nobility and fragrance of the antique world." [16] This nostalgia is merely that of the genteel museum–visitor, and Landor's nostalgia in the *Hellenics* is more complex, and more compounded with other longings.

Chrysaor (first printed in 1800) is a fragment, presented by the poet's introductory paragraph as part of a once planned epic. As in Landor's other two early poems (all three were published while he was in his early twenties), *Gebir* and *The Phocaeans*, the myth of Chrysaor is to a certain degree a vehicle for the revolutionary politics and radical religion of Landor's generation of young intellectuals. *Chrysaor* is by very far the most doctrinaire of the three poems. The republican and libertarian beliefs of those years were in many ways admirable, but as doctrine they are notoriously vague and muddled; as a result they are in themselves a handicap to the poem. The headlong enthusiasm of the time was in later years revised even by Landor, one of the most constant of the young English whose "heads were turned towards the French Revolution, and were deluded by a phantom of Liberty." [17]

In addition, this enthusiasm was one of several factors which led Landor in *Chrysaor* to attempt a grand, epic blank verse. He was ambitious; he had, always, convictions about great poetry and magnitude ("we may write little things well, and accumulate one upon another, but never will any be justly called a great poet until he has treated a great subject worthily"); [18] he was, in his early twenties, in the first ardor of a lifelong devotion to Milton; and as a result he began his career by experimenting with various kinds of heroic measure. *Chrysaor* is an interesting

16. *Ibid.*, p. 244.
17. Wheeler, *Letters*, p. 135.
18. Landor, *Works*, 4:25.

and unsuccessful attempt to adapt Milton's epic blank verse to political allegory; the influence of Milton is visible in the direct imitation of situation, conception, and verse style. (In *Gebir*, a more successful experiment, and one which Landor did complete, Milton's style also exerts a powerful influence, but as something carefully avoided.)

The distance in conception between *Chrysaor* and the *Hellenics* [19] is great. And if, as Bush maintains, this distance marks the retreat of Landor's disappointed ambition, then the retreat was unconscious. In his essay on the *Idyls* of Theocritus, in 1842, Landor not only states, but argues that the term idyll should refer to more than a pastoral museum-piece. Landor gives his (sound) etymological definition of an idyll as "a small image of something greater," and expresses his belief (less sound) that Theocritus had originally "ranged what he thought the more important and the more epic under this category." [20] In 1847, writing (in Latin) of his own *Idyllia Heroica*, Landor leaves even less doubt as to his valuation of the form; the following passage precedes the definition of the "magnae alicujus imaginis imago minor" [21] (Latin hexameter, it should be remembered, finds its traditional equivalent in English pentameter):

> People carp at the title of the Idyls, denying that they ought to be called "Heroic." That the ancients thought otherwise is clear not merely by their use of the hexameter or heroic verse-form for them, but by the sort of thing generally treated. The greater part of Theocritus, and by far the better, does not consist in the loves of shepherds and in their alternating ditties.[22]

And also in 1847, in relation to his work on the Englishing of the *Idyllia*, he wrote in a letter that "My idylls will atone for all my sins against poetry in tragedies &c &c." [23]

19. Although Landor twice published *Chrysaor* with the *Hellenics*, Bush correctly considers it as separate from the *Hellenics* or idylls proper.

20. Landor, *Works*, 13:2.

21. Landor, *Poemata et Inscriptiones* (London: Edward Moxon, 1847), p. 348.

22. *Ibid.* (translated by R. H. Super, *Walter Savage Landor*, p. 41).

23. Quoted by Super, *Walter Savage Landor*, p. 317.

Bush, with Sidney Colvin, finds "sublimity" in *Chrysaor* and proposes that the *Hellenics*, in which "Landor no longer has much to say except that young love is sweet," are "literary exercises." [24] There is a sense in which "literary exercises" is not a pejorative term; in any case, *Chrysaor* is in nearly every line suggestive of mere experiment and poetic calisthenics. Such is not true of *Gebir*, a more happy, and in fact dazzling experiment. The *Hellenics* are not in this sense experiments at all. Landor attains his most impressive blank verse, and his proper larger form, in his idylls — his peculiar lyrics-about-stories. Most of these "small images of something greater" are in the *Hellenics*, which of course include the translated *Idyllia Heroica*. In these poems, I have tried to show, the style defines the material. The style of *Chrysaor*, like all bad writing, is untrue; it attempts to make the material seem something which it is not.

Perhaps the most obvious symptom of *Chrysaor*'s systematic excess is the frequent muddiness of figure and descriptive detail, strikingly different from the hard, meticulous pictures of *Gebir* or of any poem in the *Hellenics*. *Chrysaor* is clearly the work of an extraordinary poet, but of one who is, in this poem, extraordinarily bad. Here is a Jovian gesture of ring-a-lievo:

> but the sire
> *Of mortals and immortals waved his arm*
> *Around, all all below was wild dismay:*
> *Again — 'twas agony; again — 'twas peace.*
> *lines 15–18*

Even less expected from Landor is a jumbled metaphor containing (aside from several involved personifications) fruit, furrows, animal life, a wrinkle-browed lion, and a richly guised, demon-awaking ploughman (woman?):

> *Empire bemoan I not, however shared,*
> *Nor Fortune frail, nor stubborn Fate, accuse:*
> *No! — mortals I bemoan! when Avarice,*
> *Plowing these fruitless furrows, shall awake*
> *The basking Demons, and the dormant Crimes,*

24. Bush, *Mythology and the Romantic Tradition*, p. 239.

Horrible, strong, resistless, and transform
Meekness to Madness, Patience to Despair.
What is Ambition? What but Avarice?
But Avarice in richer guize arrayed,
Stalking erect, loud-spoken, lioned-miened,
Her brow uncrost by care, but deeply markt,
And darting downwards 'twixt her eyes hard-lasht
The wrinkle of command.

lines 106–18

This passage expounds part of the poem's thin framework of ideas in an unsupportably pretentious style. The style is a function of conception, of the kind of poem which Landor is, in *Chrysaor*, trying to write. Questions of "epic" and "heroic" aside, the poem is very far in the direction of allegory. Like Milton's Adam and Satan, Shelley's Prometheus, or Keat's Hyperion, all of the characters, in all of their details, are not merely representative examples; they are in *Chrysaor* embodiments, archetypes. The following attempted set piece occurs at a pivotal moment in the poem's structure and points toward the conceptual impulse which deadens the poem's writing. Again, the reader of "Dryope," *Gebir*, or "Iphigeneia" will hardly recognize Landor in the poet whose overdrawn image is a sort of grotesque emblem for his own rhetoric. Chrysaor, the Jove-defying tyrant, has been stricken by Neptune:

his breast
Panted from consternation, and dismay,
And pride untoward, on himself o'erthrown.
From his distended nostrils issued gore,
At intervals, with which his wiry locks,
Huge arms, and bulky bosom, shone beslimed. . . .

lines 152–58

The death scene continues, still comically huge in scale, still dependent upon synonyms for "big":

No longer, bulging thro' the tempest, rose
That bulky bosom; nor those oarlike hands,
Trusted ere mortal's keenest ken conceived
The bluest shore — threw back opposing tides.
Shrunken mid brutal hair his violent veins

Subsided, yet were hideous to behold
As dragons panting in the noontide brake.
At last, absorbing deep the breath of heaven. . . .
And from a throat that as it throb'd and rose,
Seem'd shaking ponderous links of dusky iron,
Uttering one anguish-forced indignant groan,
Fired with infernal rage, the spirit flew.
                    lines 171–84

The grammatically delayed "threw back" is merely awkward, swollen rather than grand. The rest of the passage is similarly overwritten; its exaggerated devices burlesque Landor's characteristic strengths, as though the style were trying to drown out the inadequacy of statement and conception. The excessive writing of a brilliantly inventive man may be worse than the excessive writing of a merely inept man; before virtues can be abused or overextended, one must possess them. Thus, the already metaphorical chains whose heavy rattle we are supposed to hear are pointlessly visualized by the metaphorical adjective "dusky." Again, "panting" is a fine descriptive word for a reptile, but the frantically detailed realization of the dragons is based upon their very dubious resemblance to Chrysaor's veins. Even more overwrought, and less redeemed, are the mechanically clanging alliterations (keenest ken conceived, violent veins, bulky bosom, hideous to behold). In other poems, Landor yokes Latin adjectives with a homelier word and achieves descriptive precision and freshness, but here no new sense of the English potentials in a foreign root enlivens phrases like "brutal hair" and "violent veins." The concluding phrase "Fired with infernal rage" is at best redundant, at worst an aimless wordplay.

The genre of *Chrysaor*, its way of using myth, and its distance from Landor's most important mythological poems, may be indicated by a bit of jargon which also describes these stylistic gaffes: they are unsuccessful Miltonisms. In each instance, the intended force of the stylistic detail is to increase, to intensify; but this force affects only the style itself. In other settings, the devices of close realization, rhythmic intensity, classical syntax, and latinate description are Landor's in an entirely individual way, and in the service of very complex rhetorical aims. But in *Chrysaor*, where the purpose is to inflate this subject to the level of Milton's, the style becomes inadvertent parody.

In some of *Chrysaor's* lines the resemblance is sufficiently explicit for any source–detective, and probably deliberate. There is little doubt, for instance, that as Havens and Bradley say lines 200–201 are based upon lines 45 and 49, Book I, of *Paradise Lost*. More damaging than such echoes, however, is a kind of line which may not be, in fact, especially Miltonic. That is, certain elaborate devices, through overuse or unjustified use, may produce an effect which is to the reader "derivative." The tone of lofty magnificence is, exactly, *derived* from sources other than the subject, and when this is true of English blank verse which strives for epic timbre, the verse is certain to sound like bad Milton.

For example, *Chrysaor's* many epithets, including the repeated "Chrysaor, wielder of the Golden Sword" (lines 12 and 96), are annoying and mechanically literary. Yet the device is in itself less automatic, and fresher, than it might seem; often, Landor carefully arranges his Chapmanesque compound epithets in balanced pairs to construct a kind of blank-verse line which is in a way original. There is nothing wrong with the stylistic invention (see the last line of Yeats' *Byzantium*); the trouble here is that it is a stylistic invention only, a mere allusion to the compounds of Greek epic. Landor has devised a kind of line suitable to an epic which has not been written. The figure is an appeal to the prestige of Homer and Milton.

Thus, the existing poem is among other things far too short to support the number of times that this time-consuming mannerism appears:

> *Far from thy cloud-soft pillow, minion-prest,*
> *Those fleeting lassitudes that follow Love.*
> *lines 60–61*
> *His trident-sceptered brother, triton-borne.*
> *line 71*
> *The rapid-footed Rhodan, mountain-rear'd.*
> *line 90*

The Nymph-surrounded monarch of the main.
line 105
Your peace-embracing war-inciting king!
line 186

In a perversion of the "smaller picture" formula, these epic devices are crowded into a poem of slightly more than 200 lines.

Also crowded into these lines is a very large allegory supported by very little incident. The death scene comprises nearly a quarter of the poem's length; Chrysaor's speech of defiance and Jove's speech asking Neptune to destroy Chrysaor as an evidence of loyalty and obedience are both nearly as long. Character is so wooden, and plot so frail, that any outline tends to make them seem better than they are. In Iberia, Chrysaor, tyrant over men and "last of the race of earth-born giants," challenges Jove (although *how* is obscure; most of the speech is no more than back talk) in a surly, but very learned and figurative speech. The Thunderer could crush the rebel (or, rather, rebellious talker) himself, but prefers, as a token of goodwill toward his recently defeated brother Neptune, that the latter should do the work. Jove explains this, and vigorously urges Neptune to stop sulking, to give up ambition ("Ambition? 'tis unworthy of a God, / Unworthy of a brother! I am Jove, / Thou, Neptune"), and to sever Chrysaor from mankind. As Neptune makes clear in a speech which I have already quoted ("What is ambition? What but avarice?"), Jove might not have troubled, for ambition, or even "bemoaning Empire," is the furthest thing from the sea god's mind. Neptune calls his tritons, strikes one blow, and the allegedly enormous Chrysaor is instantly and like a grape squashed flat. He has from the first been ludicrously overmatched. The Iberians are punished for having endured a tyrant without rebelling. The punishment is that they must bear the new tyranny of Superstition. Daughter and last survivor of the Titans, she has been lurking in a huge black underground cave. Like every other event, this concluding "incident" is devoid not only of reason, but of interest as well.

The meaning of this allegory is confused, rather than deepened, by the contradiction between Neptune's respected docility and mankind's condemned docility. We see Chrysaor himself only in the role of a pathetically ineffective rebel, but his main importance is apparently in his role as tyrant. The poem's plot could not really interest anyone enough to care about these problems, and they are complicated by certain especially obscure lines. These lines refer to definite circumstances, such as precise lengths of time; they indicate that Super's inference is correct: "The reader has the uncomfortable suspicion that the entire poem is intended to be a close representation of the international politics of the day." [25]

Chrysaor is a wretched piece of juvenilia. Yet the poem is worth close attention, and not merely because it has been selected by distinguished critics looking for something major to point at as Landor's best work. The poem has brilliant moments, most of them moments of excess as well, at which the style tugs in a direction quite different from that of the material. *Chrysaor*, as an uncharacteristic undertaking, thus helps explain the direction of Landor's mature art. As a work of fiction tends toward allegory, its incident and character tend toward the inclusive; in an archetypal or allegorical realm everything is an embodiment, not merely an example, and no detail is merely itself. Chrysaor is meant, like Milton's Satan or Adam, or Shelley's Prometheus, to be his own significance. We are meant to accept that what such a figure does and says is meaningful, on its many levels, *because of who he is.* The plot does not simply refer to the politics of modern Europe, to those of ancient Spain, and to the principles of Rebellion and Order; the plot is, itself, all of these things.

The quality to some extent sacrificed at this level of fiction is that of contingency — simple individuality; an abstraction may be very precisely defined and may be quite a particular abstraction, but its particularity is absolutely a matter of principle, and not at all of accident. The more archetypal reality in a created world, the less intrinsic reality: as Prometheus or Satan becomes credible as the bodying forth of several abstrac-

25. Super, *Walter Savage Landor*, p. 51.

tions, he tends to depart from the realm of the actual, in which everything has a knobby, idiosyncratic reality of its own. This truism must be qualified at once by an acknowledgment that a great writer may embarrass our rules by doing nearly anything, but it is generally true that when a poet undertakes a large picture of the large meanings themselves, he has largely excluded the nominalist treatment of scenes and objects as unique, discrete instances. Once a work is committed to absolute, rather than representative, significance, it is easy to introduce a character who is Tyranny, and also George III, and also a bossy man named George Kaplan, but it is very difficult to introduce a character who is only bossy George Kaplan, whose actions are not momentous in themselves. Once absolute significance is asserted, it cannot easily be evaded.

This is a matter of literary form, and not of breadth of subject: George Kaplan may raise quite as many serious issues as Tyranny–George III–Kaplan. And Landor's preoccupations and talents led him toward literary forms based upon the singularity of the particular thing, its remoteness from the realm of absolutes. The stylistic capacity for close visualization of physical detail is a presiding source of energy in the *Hellenics*; in *Chrysaor* it is misused in an attempt to inflate an inadequate hero. One kind of descriptive power can render a storm which is, predominantly, the wrath of Satan, and this power is Milton's; Landor's power, irrelevant to the mode of *Chrysaor*, is, predominantly, to strike us with wonder that each moment of this storm is like no other, that this storm is unique, passing, and real. Landor himself wrote sensibly of his more successful early poems:

> the language of *Paradise Lost* ought not to be the language of *Gebir*. There should be the softened air of remote antiquity, not the severe air of unapproachable sanctity.[26]

Furthermore, Landor's style itself, dependent as it is upon the small variation rather than the grand one, is unsuited to the venture of *Chrysaor*.

26. Landor, *Works*, 13:351.

In the matter of character, no less than in style, Landor's mature achievement is far removed from anything like allegory. Drimacos leads a successful slave revolt, but his actions are important only as notable examples, out of thousands, of certain noble qualities — and as examples they are nearly forgotten. The seduction of Dryope is not important because Apollo is the Spirit of Creativity (or something) and Dryope is Mankind. Apollo's action in the poem is, precisely, to withhold, while displaying, his mysterious being as the embodiment of absolute qualities. He changes, shimmers, evades. The emphasis is upon this seduction as one of innumerable visitations, and upon our knowledge of the Sun as very small, at best. If Dryope "symbolizes" anything, it is not Mankind, but One of Mankind.

Indeed, the contents page of any edition of the *Hellenics* shows that Landor usually chooses obscure names rather than Olympian ones; often the character on whom he builds a poem came to him as little more than a name. (In *less* ambitious poems like the dramatic scenes, this is slightly less true.) Sometimes, Ulysses or Apollo or Helen will appear, but as something singular, as a figure briefly midway between the mundane and the mythical: Apollo descends, Ulysses is an old man in Italy, about to die, Helen is an adolescent nearly deflowered by a roguish Theseus.

More often, in shaping a poem Landor appears to have begun with the singular, primitive scene and developed the aura of permanence or significance. Perhaps we can describe the quality achieved by either method as heroic rather than epic. In either case, the actual event does not function as the author's created expression of a metaphysical or psychological vision; rather, the event acquires the quality of something given, inherited, and unchangeable. This remove from anything like allegory is necessary to the recurrent theme of the mythical as opposed to the passionate. The teller is preoccupied with the calm of time and the disquiet of event which together are the myth, and so the myth, because its essence is to come from without, cannot epitomize any mere statement of the teller.

Rather than allegorize, then, Landor maintains Idea, the referent of allegory, as forever verging upon the manifest, forever intimated as part of the "something larger" of which the poem is an image. If we consider allegory as a Platonic technique, then Landor is the man who will not leave the Cave, although he will assert — and persuade — that it is a Cave. In other words, he is by temperament a skeptic — too complete and honest a skeptic to make a successful allegorist. This skepticism is an emotion rather than an intellectual principle; it causes (and perhaps also results from) an inability to deal, in poetry, with certain kinds of abstract thought.

That this abstention from what Landor snorted at as "metaphysics" is to the good, we can judge from the miserable failure of *Chrysaor*, in which abstractions are equally muddled whether they appear as capitalized nouns, as characters, or as both. The world of real forms outside the cave is merely asserted. Confusion of thought, which is a vice even in prose, is overlooked in *Chrysaor* by Colvin and also by Bush. In an early chapter of his book the latter finds it no weakness in *The Witch of Atlas* or *Prometheus Unbound* that these poems are almost completely obscure "endless puzzles" with, probably, no intended answers. The Witch is earthly love, and also heavenly love, and also the Poetic Imagination:

> Shelley touches a name, awakens an association, and skims on his winged way. The witch is related to the One of Shelley's Platonic heaven, but here, as often in more serious poems, he is most poetically satisfying when he is flitting, a radiant butterfly, among the Many.[27]

It is worth noticing that Bush's defense (or rather praise) of Shelley's obscurity includes the statement that Shelley, by "playing by himself in public," "anticipates poets of our time." [28] Post-Romantic poetry (and pedagogy) has indeed furthered the equation of poetic complexity with multiplicity of association, and of poetic ambition with a splendid obscurity. The virtue

27. Bush, *Mythology and the Romantic Tradition*, p. 143.
28. *Ibid.*, p. 139.

of ambiguity has almost completely crowded the virtue of clarity out of our poetic; to tell a man that his poems are clear is an insult: who would ever write a dissertation about them?

There is little wonder, then, that charitable scholars should attempt to rest Landor's reputation upon *Chrysaor*. The emotional complexity of his major poems is communicated by clarity of definition. Such definition arises from the choices of style — innumerable small exclusions, rather than awakenings, of association.

The Landor who abandoned the mode of *Chrysaor* of course knew all of this about his own art and about the opposite tide of contemporary poetry; there is more than a little of pride, polemic, and snootiness in the verse "Apology for the *Hellenics*" ("Fantastic forms weak minds invent"). A four-sentence preface to the 1859 *Hellenics* states the opposition between multiplicity and clarity most concisely:

> Little in these pages will gratify the generality of readers. Poetry, in our day, is oftener prismatic than diaphanous: this is not so: they who look into it may see through. If there be anywhere a few small air bubbles, it yet leaves to the clear vision a wide expanse of varied scenery.

And even more explicit crotchet is put in the mouth of Southey in the second imaginary conversation of "Southey and Porson":

> What a blessing are metaphysics to our generation! A poet or other who can make nothing clear can stir up enough sediment to render the bottom of a basin as invisible as the deepest gulf in the Atlantic. The shallowest pond, if turbid, has depth enough for a goose to hide its head in.[29]

The hauteur and the implied self-defense are of course not Southey's, but Landor's.

In a mythological allegory like *Chrysaor*, any air of mystery refers the reader to the world of abstract significance implying a verbal "meaning." To say that Landor, in the *Hellenics*, treats myth *as myth* means that he is interested in the events and emotions themselves, and as they are touched by the mys-

29. Landor, *Works*, 5:198.

tery of permanence, of myth itself. His characters are human beings, but they are also more than human beings, slightly enlarged, beyond life, like heroic statues. They are a means of expressing fascination with human emotion as it is stylized by the processes of time, narration, and cognition. The distinction between the mystery of *The Witch of Atlas* and the mystery in "Dryope" is contained in the concept of clarity: the refusal, in the face of wonder, to imply a known, withheld significance. What is known of Apollo is told, and the rest is frank awe.

Occasional Poems

I have been saying that Landor at his best often uses a frankly literary, introspective technique in order to reilluminate a stock sentiment or a mythological incident. A self-conscious interest in his own psychology as poet similarly deepens several of his many poems written in response to a particular event or situation. As with commonplace and myth, Landor builds toward personal statement from the literary decorum traditionally proper to the occasion. For an occasion, like a landscape or a moment of history, could inspire his concern with the gap between the mind and the thing conceived. But before examining the deepening of occasional poetry into something greater, I should like to honor certain of Landor's occasional poems for what they are: supreme models in a modest genre.

Landor is a delightful and heartening figure for contemplation partly because he was so at home in verse, sometimes virtually thinking and responding in it. The *Works* display poems on birthdays, weddings, revolutions, deaths of people and animals, elections, journeys, separations, meetings, and brief encounters with trees, birds, children, and politicians. I think that it will pay to begin at the very bottom of this category, at the most slight level: in his late eighties, having just left Mrs. Landor and his beloved Fiesole for the final time, he was chortling over a couplet which he recited for the Brownings but never published, one little verse recorded of the many which he tells us he burned:

> *An angel from his Paradise drove Adam;*
> *From mine a devil drove me — thank you, Madam.*[30]

This facility, although we tend to dismiss such matters, was an important part of the man's mind. That Landor broke into doggerel or good couplets while talking with friends indicates only an obsession, not unique, with iambs and rhymes. But the relationship of iambic rhythm, in Landor's mind, with prose composition indicates that he believed in the taut, assured tone of verse itself, the tone of all verse, in whose presence he lived. This can be said, perhaps, of all poets, or of all great ones, but in Landor's sensibility there is the special element of his concern with experience as an elusive, crude donnée, and with style as a personal means toward the refinement of knowledge. He wrote occasional poems because verse was the mode of knowledge in which he had most confidence, and which his mind — naturally, in a sense — demanded. That demand is dramatized by the pressure of iambic rhythm — which he also knew how to *avoid* — upon his prose reading and writing.

First, the reading: in preparation for a sly critical *tour de force*, Landor digresses from his essay "The Poems of Catullus" to criticize Hallam for calling the following verses from *Paradise Regained* (book iii, line 337) "perhaps the most musical verses Milton has ever produced." As Landor says, "They are these (*si diis placet!*)":

> *Such forces met not, nor so wide a camp,*
> *When Agrican with all his northern powers*
> *Besieged Albracca, as romances tell,*
> *The city of Gallaphrone, from thence to win*
> *The fairest of her sex Angelica*
> *His daughter, sought by many prowest knights,*
> *Both Paynim and the peers of Charlemagne.*[31]

30. Browning helped improve the lines and gets credit for the rhyme. See Super, *Walter Savage Landor*, p. 472.
31. Landor, *Works*, 11:188.

Landor grants the verses fluency, apart from the "sad hiatus" of "Albracca as"; he then observes the prosy feebleness in "thought and expression" of these verses "unluckily hit upon for harmony," concluding that Hallam was eager to praise "that which nobody ever praised before." The essay moves on toward a comparison of the heroic measures of Milton and Catullus, and Hallam's passage has apparently served its purpose by substantiating Landor's earlier remark: "There is many a critic who talks of harmony, and whose ear seems to have been fashioned out of the callus of his foot."

On the next page, however, the passage is referred to again: Landor finds verses "more harmonious," and in an unlikely part of Milton's work. "But what magnificence of thought is here! How totally free is the expression from the encumbrances of amplification, from the crutches and cushions of swollen feebleness!"

> *When God commands to take the trumpet*
> *And blow a shriller and a louder blast,*
> *It rests not in Man's will what he shall do,*
> *Or what he shall forbear.*

It is important to note how interested Landor is, how much he is enjoying himself. He continues, "This sentence in the *Treatise on Prelaty* is printed in prose: it sounds like inspiration. 'It rested not in Milton's will' to crack his organ-pipe, for the sake of splitting and attenuating the gush of harmony."

That is, the quality of verse-harmony is nearly indistinguishable from a certain kind of verbal inspiration. The opinion would be less remarkable if Landor were not such a scientific student of quantity, accent, consonant-value, and line: "harmony" is here spoken of as an objective quality in verse, although as a quality which is unattainable without a certain subjective intensity of thought. Further, iambic harmony is sometimes irresistible to a poet who is thinking at the level most removed from "feebleness." Landor's exultant applause shows how much the idea absorbs him. And the converse of the idea is that when a fragment of experience is given iambic harmony, authentic harmony free from crutches, cushions, and amplification, then that experience is elevated. If the poet can manage the stylistic problem, the experience is grasped as few things can be. Therefore, any available subject which one can conceive in verse is valid quarry: "Regarding the occasional in poetry: is there less merit in taking and treating what is before us, than in seeking and wandering through an open field as we would for mushrooms?"[32]

It is no surprise, then, to find Landor writing to Forster of his own work:

> While writing the Tancredi and Constantia dialogue, I had the greatest difficulty to prevent my prose running away with me. Sundry verses indeed I could not keep down, nor could I afterwards break into prose. Here is a specimen, not in the conversation as it stands at present, which was written while I fancied I was writing Prose:
>
> *Can certain words pronounced by certain men*
> *Perform an incantation which shall hold*
> *Two hearts together to the end of time?*
> *If these were wanting, yet instead of these*
> *There was my father's word, and there was God.*

These lines are printed by Wheeler in the *Works* along with other fragments of inadvertent, unmistakable verse. On the facing page, also tucked in with with short poems not published by Landor, is an offhand statement of his remarkable faith in the tonal complexities and compressions of verse rhythm:

> ### Epigrams
>
> *Epigrams must be curt, nor seem*
> *Tail-pieces to a poet's dream.*
> *If they should anywhere be found*
> *Serious, or musical in sound*
> *Turn into prose the two worst pages*
> *And you will rank among the sages.*

That is not itself a great epigram, but it is not quite a jingle either, for no jingler would disturb his work with the extraor-

32. *Ibid.*, 6:41.

dinary assertion embedded in the word "or" of the fourth line. The true music of verse, says Landor, can lend a condensed profundity of tone which, if it could be paraphrased, would yield prose of classic penetration: again the faith may be common to all poets, but it is especially Landor's. No matter what sort of rhyming he toyed with, he felt himself to be practicing in a solemnly magic art.

Progressing upward through the kinds of Landor's occasional poetry, from inadvertent blank verse and the gibe at Mrs. Landor, a suitable occasion, in the strict sense, is Landor's meeting with Wordsworth in June, 1832. An older Wordsworth, as Poet Laureate, would later refer to Landor as a man "deplorably tormented by ungovernable passion . . . a madman, a bad-man, yet a man of genius, as many a madman is." [33] But on this first meeting, Wordsworth established a great and mutual liking for Landor, whom he had already called "a Poet who has written verses of which I would rather have been the Author than of any produced in our time." [34] Called upon to write some lines in Dora Wordsworth's album, which was heavy with celebrated names, Landor wrote eight lines which must comprise the best album-poem ever written entirely within the confines of the type. He even includes a fine eighteenth-century line which neatly distinguishes, and suitably compliments, father and daughter — personification at its most light and *juste:*

For Miss Wordsworth's Album, At Wordsworth's Desire

> *Glorious the names that cluster here,*
> *The loftiest of our lofty ile;*
> *Who can approach them void of fear,*
> *Though Genius urge & Friendship smile?*
>
> *To lay one stone upon the hill,*
> *And shew that I have climbed so high,*
> *Is what they bid me. Wordsworth's will*
> *Is law, and Landor must comply.*

The lines are short, credibly complimentary, and absolutely fitted to the particular situation; they refer to the volume

33. Quoted by Super, *Walter Savage Landor*, p. 344.
34. *Ibid.*, p. 152.

itself and to each of the people involved. The flattery is reasonable and maintains its quality of sincerity because both tropes — the personification and the hill-metaphor — are beautifully handled without fuss or involution.

These graces point toward Landor's more ambitious use of a personal or social situation as the rhetorical base for a poem, but in valuing such poems as "At Wordsworth's Desire" for themselves, one should recall Davie's appeal to urbanity as the quality of speaking for an *urbs*. Urbane diction and statement, according to that definition, affirm by their tone the grasp of life attained in a center of thought and culture. Rome, or Paris, or the court, embodies "the best" in taste and thought, and so, according to the Arnoldian definition, urbane poetry can bear "the best" as a message. Landor, a warmly literary man to the heart, loved to make such poems, and would often devise or assume a situation (in the following case a stock one, in fact), as in this imitation of Catullus (Carmen XXI.1):

Old Style

Aurelius, Sire of Hungrinesses!
Thee thy old friend Catullus blesses,
And sends thee six fine watercresses.

There are who would not think me quite
(Unless we were old friends) polite
To mention whom you should invite.

Look at them well; and turn it o'er
In your own mind . . I'd have but four . .
Lucullus, Caesar, and two more.

The poem is not of Rome or London. But it does bear a message of judging urbanely — "Look at them well" — in all things: cresses, manners, wit, men, and music. Music, because the first triplet wins us over at once by joyfully striking tune from three hissing consonant-sounds, a few syncopated vowels, and an impossible rhyme. It should be impossible to read such verse without happy admiration for the English tongue, as well as for poets Latin and English, for friendship, for the making of distinctions, and even for watercresses.

The elation of "Old Style" is that of discovering an *urbs* — a center of "looking at them well" — which is timeless, placeless, and unaffected. Catullus, Aurelius, Landor — and oneself: the community inspires admiration partly because of what it transcends, yet the citizens are not too disembodied to appreciate good farm produce. But Landor is an intensely personal poet in a quite literal sense, and another group of what may be called occasional poems constitute an intimate verse journal, his most satisfying biography. The need for a starting point, for a crudely defined and fictional situation, probably motivated imitations like "Old Style" as well as some of Landor's apparently "dramatic" forms — dialogues, dramatic scenes, and peculiar non-plays. At the same time, he again and again responded with a short poem to important or symbolic occasions in his own life. The moment may be fragile, as in "The Death of Day" ("My pictures blacken in their frames") or as formal as epitaph. Dozens of poems are addressed to Ianthe (Jane Swift), the forbidden, unattained love of Landor's long life, and these poems lend one another force, culminating in the moving poem "Memory" when Landor confronts the decaying recall of old age: he speaks with terror of the moments when he can recall only her name, nothing else, and nothing else of her. Her image always, however, returns "called or uncalled," and this affirmation gathers enormous force from the preceding seventy years of "occasional" poems; we recall his epigram on the emblem of her name:

> *One lovely name adorns my song,*
> *And, dwelling in the heart,*
> *Forever falters at the tongue,*
> *And trembles to depart.*

These many poems addressed to Ianthe, or about her, also contribute to the power of certain occasional poems which only have something to do with her. Whether an epitaph is strictly an occasional poem or not, the following lines belong in the category; they grow from a very particular circumstance and an actual occasion. When Ianthe and Landor met in Italy after many years, each had children. Soon, she and her daughters helped him plant a certain plot near his villa.

For An Epitaph at Fiesole

Lo! where the four mimosas blend their shade,
In calm repose at last is Landor laid;
For ere he slept he saw them planted here
By her his soul had ever held most dear,
And he had lived enough when he had dried her tear.

The poem is an emotional balance between a particular, real situation and a general, artificial one. Wordsworth, I have suggested much earlier, desires for his purposes an impression of authenticity even for a completely fictional experience; Landor, even in occasional or autobiographical poems, reverses the process somewhat. In the "Epitaph at Fiesole," Landor naturally reaches toward an archetypal occasion, and toward a traditional literary form, while maintaining the features of his unique, actual experience. Instead of writing a school-piece, or a little poem which might be obscure without a close knowledge of the poet's life, he shaped an incident of his life (which he indeed lived poetically) so that the incident takes on the feeling of a traditional, immutable form. The lines in Dora Wordsworth's album comprise an excellent album-poem because they particularize the occasion absolutely, yet remain within the bounds of the genre. Similarly, the epitaph evokes the flavor of a particular relationship, yet remains substantially an epitaph.

The verse-movement of the five lines, then, reflects the balance between personal statement and formal epitaph; since the poem is short and simple, it also provides a good opportunity to study Landor's metrical practice in detail. It is largely by effects of rhythm that he manages to combine the formal with the intimate. The devices include a reliance upon one- and two-syllable words, a slow line, and a use of the strict line-ending to develop emotion in successive, increasing stages. The first two lines are a complete formal epitaph within the whole; from the first syllable, which marks the only substitution for an iambic foot, this closed couplet proceeds with accent reinforced, in every foot, by quantity. The slowing produced by this reinforcement is furthered by calm monosyllables and by the position of the disyllable "repose," which (unlike, for example, "Landor" and "planted") delimits one foot rather than linking two. The line ending of this couplet occurs at the exact logical division; and in all the opening statement, relieved only by a slight acceleration upon "mimosa," is very final, unhurried, and ceremonious — as is the diction, moving from a frank archaism to the standard verb of all epitaph in all languages. The next (third) line is similar in movement, but lighter because quantity does not especially emphasize the ictus, and because of the position given to the one disyllable. Furthermore, the jointure of this couplet, relative to that of the preceding one, is a runover.

The statement, it is very clear, correspondingly becomes less formal and more personal; although remaining in the third person, the epitaph has become more intimate. This couplet like the first begins with an archaism ("ere") just as it also contains monosyllables, and the conventionality of "laid" is echoed by the impersonal near-cliché "he slept," but the action of planting and the phrase "most dear" partially relax the original stateliness of diction. Each of the third and fourth lines increases the intimacy and intensity of feeling, as does the second couplet as a unit, but the greatest furthering of emotion comes with the final (fifth) line, after the poem has reached its second internal close of logic, tone, and rhythm. The sentiment of the final line would be sentimental if the line did not grow naturally out of the contrasting restraint of the beginning.

The tonal rightness of that growth, and the poem's soundness as a whole, is largely the result of rhythm, especially the remarkable rhythm of the final hexameter line. The poem accelerates very gradually through four lines of slow pentameter, and in those lines all five accents are quite full, and quite clearly more accented than any unaccented syllable in the line: in other words, they contain five accents (relative to the line) as well as five stresses (relative to the other syllable in the foot). The last line represents a somewhat unexpected spill into the poet's full emotion, almost as a nearly suppressed afterthought, and this burst is reflected by the change to hexameter. But the long last line's movement is successfully knitted to that of the preceding four by several means: the hexameter, a difficult measure in English, is divided in half, and each half begins with a weak accent, the word "he" being further deemphasized by grammatical parallelism; thus, the long line has only four strong accents, blending it with the five-accent pentameters. But although the line of accelerated feeling is also quicker in movement, especially in its first half, it repeats certain motifs of the poem's somber beginning. That is, it returns to the second line's treatment of the one disyllabic word, marking rather than bridging the foot division. This disyllable coincides with the very pronounced caesura, so that the line of two quick halves (the first less so than the second) is fairly slow as a whole even though it deemphasizes two of its stresses. Usually, a diminished accent quickens a line; by countering this tendency, Landor achieves much more variation than might be expected within the poem's norm of the slow line.

Such metrical analysis is a rough descriptive approximation. It is not what should pass through one's mind as he reads this or any poem, but it may begin to isolate some of the reasons why a poem like "For An Epitaph At Fiesole" appeals so greatly. We may be apt to doubt our own attraction to a poem which speaks of drying tears and of being laid in calm repose. Conventional language is one of the rules by which Landor sometimes played, and the role of things conventional in this poem is a moving one. Brilliant exploitation of conventional language is perhaps even more difficult to detect than brilliant departures from it; one of the reasons why Landor's poems outlast thousands which used similar language is his ability to establish a persuasive, congruent setting for the conventional. A powerful aspect of that setting is his metrical achievement; the poem must be heard.

Another aspect of Landor's art, of course, is that he usually had his eye trained upon a genuine subject: he does not insert tears which are meant simply to be picturesque. A poem of more than thirty years later helps to illustrate the way in which Landor's epigrams lend one another momentum, as entries in an intense, careworked journal. Ianthe dead, Landor is an exile from his villa, a Lear estranged from his genuinely awful first-born, Arnold:

> *Never must my bones be laid*
> *Under the mimosa's shade.*
> *He to whom I gave my all*
> *Swept away her guardian wall,*
> *And her green and level plot*
> *Green or level now is not.*

The epigram, for Landor, was a form by which the particular circumstances of life might attain a cool, changeless verity. The feeling can be retained as itself, unadorned by wit, partly because the form is short; these lines defy the charge of excessive sentimentality because they are plain to the explicit bone, and because their form is as modest as it is irreducible.

Not all of the poems which proceed from an actual circumstance are epigrams, nor, epigrams or not, do they remain modestly occasional even in the sense that most of the Ianthe-poems are occasional. Landor had an obsessive, skeptic's concern with the most traditional of subjects, the tyranny of time; frequently, a given circumstance is illuminated by the paradoxical nature of any given moment: in it, we cannot escape it, and when it is past, we cannot penetrate its irrevocable, oblivious quiet. Landor's deep attraction toward the "other," as embodied in the past or in mute particulars, is intimated in one of the most famous epigrams. (The occasion could not be more specific: Leigh Hunt showed Landor a single strand of Lucretia Borgia's hair, stolen by Byron or Trelawny from a museum in Milan.) [35]

35. As Super speculates in *Walter Savage Landor*, p. 178.

On Seeing A Hair of Lucretia Borgia

Borgia, thou once wert almost too august,
And high for adoration; — now thou'rt dust!
All that remains of thee these plaits unfold —
Calm hair, meandering with pellucid gold!

The traditional theme is here strangely changed. The bright curve indicates that Borgia, once grand, is dust, but it also emblemizes an absolute grandeur in death of which her life was merely an augur. Augur: august, august: Augustus — the conventional vocabulary is chosen and disposed with care, and produces an effect which idiosyncratic or obviously "fresh" diction could not. That effect is urbanity; the loveliness and power generated in a few lines combines our wonder at the gorgeous, dead apparition which is the hair with our wonder at the quiet splendor of the statement itself. That two rhymes and a varying caesura can do so much produces an emotion analogous to that caused by the hair. The rhymes are fresh, hard, and inevitable, yet the words in the rhymes are conventional. The movement of the last line, like the pellucid gold itself, affirms how much energy may be contained in quiet — quiet shadowed by the past. In a way difficult of paraphrase, the theme of distance and of *ubi sunt* loses some of its pessimism; the relief from pessimism is neither religious nor stoic, but consists of Romantic awe before the serene, suggestive artifact.

That feeling, which can be called Romantic for the want of a better term, hovers about the lines on Lucretia Borgia. It is a response to the relationship between an absolutely particular perception and the contrasting absolute of time. Before showing how similar concerns transform a longer occasional poem, "To My Child Carlino," it may help to note a more explicit poetic statement of the theme.

I have suggested that Landor's reaction to a particular occasion is colored by a special perception of what an occasion is: each occasion constitutes an isolated problem in how to respond, and as such it is in some ways like (though also unlike!) a rhetorical topic: my epitaph must be true to the nature of a traditional occasion and to the nature of a unique occasion. Each of these occasions for response presents a challenging, obdurate donnée, and the intense rhetorical problem of what tone to take is also a pressing ethical problem. This dual problem of the traditional and the unique, the rhetorical and the personal, applies even to seemingly impersonal and artificial situations like Borgia's hair. One of the most compelling aspects of that subject is the sense of Borgia as a particular, historical woman, and the hair as a particular, inscrutable object. Parallel to this distinction between the recalled past and the observed fact is the distinction between the traditional theme of "all that remains" and the more personal admiration for the hair's serenity.

This compound fascination is not simply a restatement of mutability, the *memento mori*, or the melancholy of passing time. No cliché adequately describes Landor's special concern with the theme of time. In "On Music," a poem which states that special concern explicitly, clichés are played against the rather surprising final statement. Music is one of Landor's favorite metaphors for the passing moment which can be understood only in the context of time which also removes us from the moment; in his prose he speaks of the single note whose meaning is dependent upon the notes which it supplants and which supplant it.[36]

The first quatrain of "On Music" seems a graceful enough statement of an ordinary sentiment; the runover in the second line is very nice: [37]

> *Many love music but for music's sake,*
> *Many because her touches can awake*

36. "Aesop and Rhodope," *Works,* 1:15:
> the present, like a note in music, is nothing but as it appertains to what is past and what is to come.

"Fra Filippo Lippi and Pope Eugenius IV," *Works,* 2:302:
> A bell warbles the more mellifluously in the air when the sound of the stroke is over, and when another swims out from underneath it, and pants upon the element that gave it birth.

37. An uninterrupted text of "On Music" and one of "To My Child Carlino" are printed at the end of this chapter (pp. 115–16).

> *Thoughts that repose within the breast half-dead,*
> *And rise to follow where she loves to lead.*

The following, middle lines appear, the first time through, to repeat needlessly something already said with more taste; their diction is worn, conventional in the worst sense, and after the opening four-line sentence this couplet seems the more inadequate because of its end-stopped structure:

> *What various feelings come from days gone by!*
> *What tears from far-off sources dim the eye!*

The predictably dim eye resembles the flowing numbers of Wordsworth's lines:

> *Will no one tell me what she sings? —*
> *Perhaps the plaintive numbers flow*
> *For old, unhappy, far-off things,*
> *And battles long ago:*
> *Or is it some more humble lay,*
> *Familiar matter of to-day?*
> *Some natural sorrow, loss or pain,*
> *That has been, and may be again?*

But Landor's couplet, besides being shorter than Wordsworth's stanza, is ironic. If two one-sentence quatrains divided by an end-stopped couplet, with the whole rhyming in couplets, comprised a fixed form, like the sonnet, then Landor's poem would serve to exemplify the structural capacities of the form. The first word of the closing quatrain, like the opening of a sestet, announces the turn of meaning:

> *Few, when light fingers with sweet voices play*
> *And melodies swell, pause, and melt away,*
> *Mind how at every touch, at every tone,*
> *A spark of life hath glisten'd and hath gone.*

Nearly everyone, that is, can love music as itself, as the piece which one hears; nearly everyone can love music as revery because it enables one to abstract nostalgic feelings and memories from the heard fact. What few realize is the further meaning of music, any music, in itself: its loveliness is mutable, not incidentally, but *in essence*. Music, by its nature, passes, and so inevitably reflects on life; those who only "love music but for music's sake" do not, therefore, really love it with complete understanding. Like those whose reaction is limited to that of the intermediate couplet, they love, they are on the right track, but they are not yet "minding" everything. The passing life of "every touch, every tone" is not merely mutable: in feeling, these lines combine mutability with eternal, esthetic calm in a single metaphor. All melody is the immutable emblem of change. Distance and the pasage of time, which make things beautiful and decorous, also make them painful, because beyond recall. The poem, like so much Romantic art, deals with the two edges of the word "inviolate."

To allegorize: many people can appreciate for itself a given, conventional aspect of experience (orange blossoms; a green graveplot and my dear, now closing relationship with Ianthe; the hair as emblem of decay). Few, however, go beyond these stages to realize the paradoxical nature of all isolate occasions: by coming only once, they attain as they pass the impenetrable, glistening beauty of what is unique (the particular blossom falling, my love for Ianthe summarized in a final epitaph, the particular hair embodying the changeless allure of the past). The Romantic, nostalgic perception of the middle lines is not rejected as an attitude toward experience. Rather, it is qualified — both rhythmically and explicitly — as being wooden and incomplete. The incompletion is demonstrated by a contrasting, masterful evocation of music in the final four-line unit: in the pauses of the second line, in the trochaic substitution on the delayed verb "Mind," and in the imitative pace of the final line, ending effectively on the long syllable "gone."

Landor goes from a statement of the object to an extrapolation of feeling, and then back away from the so-called pathetic fallacy to a greater awareness of the object itself, the unmoving core of its own varying associations. The emphasis is upon the final realization of the music itself, as a thing which is never "but for its own sake." It is interesting to compare those four lines with the whole presentation of music by Wordsworth in "The Solitary Reaper"; his closest attempt at virtual description of the song is in two lines which relate the music to the landscape:

> *O listen! for the Vale profound*
> *Is overflowing with the sound.*

Wordsworth's poem really concerns the revery inspired by the music, the musician, and the scene — not the music. The music's importance is merely causal in the stanza already quoted, and in the other "descriptive" stanzas:

> *No Nightingale did ever chaunt*
> *More welcome notes to weary bands*
> *Or travellers in some shady haunt,*
> *Among arabian sands:*
> *A voice so thrilling ne'er was heard*
> *In spring-time from the Cuckoo-bird,*
> *Breaking the silence of the seas*
> *Among the farthest Hebrides.*

Landor is content to say that music inspires revery and rises to a detailed emphasis upon the exact nature of music itself, defining — largely by his own style — the process of its emotional effect. Wordsworth is content to say that the music is there, and rises to a detailed emphasis upon the quality of his revery, defining that quality largely by an attempted portrayal of the exact, particular occasion.

Battles long ago, "some" shady haunt, desert nightingales, and island cuckoos are (I take it) all meant to suggest this particular revery. The vagueness and uncertainty of the actual experience constitutes most of its value for Wordsworth, who in fact climbs the hill before the song is over, rather than approaching the singer so as to hear the words and so make clear the whole process. (Indeed, Wordsworth's grammar consciously or unconsciously implies that memory of the revery obliterates memory of the barely heard song almost immediately: he "long bore" the music in his heart only *as* he mounted the hill.) Landor's opposite interests, in the actual process and in his own act of perception, mark the distinction between the occasion as real incident, leading to nostalgia, and the occasion as rhetorical starting point for definition.

When Walt Whitman leaves the learned astronomer with his charts and graphs, and goes outside to muse upon the night sky, he follows the established path of Wordsworth. However, the supposition that everything is Romantic or Classic fails here: Landor in the right mood might have stayed inside and listened with fascination to an account of the timeless tracks of the world-circled, far-off suns, but he would be likely to incorporate some of the information into a quite Romantic lyric about the mythical constellations which, cool and changeless to the eye, burn ceaselessly with heroic light.

I think that a comparison of "On Music" with "The Solitary Reaper" (and the comparison can be extended further) calls into doubt an automatic valuing of Wordsworth's discoveries over Landor's reconsiderations. It is doubtful whether any poet ever truly discovers any new thought other than his exact words; no brilliant paraphrase will ever prove Shakespeare's originality, which rests upon the exact orchestrations of thought and emotion which he made. Aside from this consideration, and whether one prefers Wordsworth's poem or Landor's, there is little doubt that Wordsworth, approaching a unique experience in a specialized stanzaic form, achieves the restatement of a very familiar, general creed. Landor undertakes a conventional subject, in pentameter couplets. He achieves the statement of a special, personal creed which would startle if the poem were managed less deftly. The creed consists of an emotional commitment to the particular occasion or experience as something lost, moving into distance, but nevertheless demanding intense pursuit. In this pursuit, revery is both a needful stage and, finally, an evasion.

Revery, a painful sense of distance, and the development of an occasion into the base for an introspective statement all characterize Landor's poem "To My Child Carlino." As the "Fiesolan Idyl" qualifies Romantic animation of nature, this poem qualifies Romantic distrust of adult intelligence. As in the Ianthe-epitaph, Landor combines a traditional poetic topic — call it the Exile's Missive [38] — with a highly particularized intimate situation: Walter Savage Landor writes from England to the son in Italy from whom he has been separated.

The poem is rich in specified domestic details, yet, characteristically, Landor first published it as part of *The Pentameron*. There it is presented as a manuscript which Boccaccio happens to have about the house, written by "a gentleman who resided long in this country." This balance between the timeless and the grainily specific, the conventional and the actual, is one of Landor's most basic ideals; Petrarca states it elsewhere when Boccaccio offers a true anecdote to his friend:

> Petrarca. Relate it to me, Messer Giovanni; for you are able to give reality the merits and charms of fiction, just as easily as you give fiction the semblance, the stature, and the movement of reality.[39]

Thus, in the conversation of Dante and Beatrice, Dante composes some lines in response to Beatrice's engagement; they are later published by Landor with the title "To Ianthe." In the same way, "To My Child Carlino" treats Landor's exile from Italy with autobiographical depth, but maintains its impeccable detachment to the extent of serving as a fourteenth-century poem. This double quality represents the best ideals of neo-Classicism, but, because of Landor's special concerns (with certain Romantic themes, and with the conventional as it transforms the personal), it also represents much more.

Landor had left Fiesole for England because he could not live with his wife, nor she with him. All that one truly needs to know of the situation is what Boccaccio tells us. "They are verses written by a gentleman who resided long in this country, and who much regretted the necessity of leaving it." The poem establishes its own dramatic situation at once: [40]

38. E.g., Ovid's *Tristia*.
39. Landor, *Works*, 2:235.
40. See the end of this chapter for an uninterrupted text.

> *Carlino! what art thou about, my boy?*
> *Often I ask that question, though in vain;*
> *For we are far apart: ah! therefore 'tis*
> *I often ask it; not in such a tone*
> *As wiser fathers do, who know too well.*
> *Were we not children, you and I together?*

But they were not children together. These apparently simple lines also establish several of the poem's complex themes: the father is far from the son, far from innocence, and also far, it will appear, from the world of natural particulars in which the boy still moves. The son is far from wisdom, but the father, for whom wisdom has been bitter, also feels — or would like to feel — less wise than other men. The poem so far appears in many ways to be a rather blatant, watery-eyed version of the Romantic attitude toward childhood and children: they are happy, wise-in-ignorance, and superior to us because more leisured, less intelligent, and generally closer to unconscious, benevolent nature.

But in fact the poem, although certainly about the man's wistful mood and not about fatherhood or the child's life, cuts against this innocent irrationalism. Landor in his ache for peace would like to escape from wisdom, but he knows that this escape is impossible, that children are often foolish and cruel, that they would benefit by wisdom. He also knows that nature is harsh, its only "wisdom" oblivion. Yet he does feel the impossible and even dangerous desire to lose his painful adult consciousness in the smaller world of sensory experience. He would like to be small, and the temptation is made very beautiful. Nevertheless, it is finally made frightening; the series of vignettes which comprise most of these fifty-eight lines are so many radical contradictions of the familiar, wistful statement (lines 35–36):

> *For thy pure breast*
> *I have no lesson; it for me has many.*

The natural details in which Landor would immerse himself are also the means by which the immersion is criticized; he sees too clearly. This situation produces a very powerful emotion, a chord strengthened by the genuine sense of plain lonesomeness for home and for the boy.

The first vignette begins with trust; the pastoral softness of a favorite rustic bench, a gift which has crossed the distance, and some speculated affection. But the scene closes with (Freudian) destruction, guilt, and an unexpected chill symbolized by some lovely flowers turned to a symbol of shame and hostile accusation:

> *Well could we trust each other. Tell me then*
> *What thou art doing. Carving out thy name,*
> *Or haply mine, upon my favourite seat,*
> *With the new knife I sent thee over sea?*
> *Or hast thou broken it, and is the hilt*
> *Among the myrtles, starr'd with flowers, behind?*
> *Or under that high throne whence fifty lilies*
> *(With sworded tuberoses dense around)*
> *Lift up their heads at once . . . not without fear*
> *That they were looking at thee all the while.*

The fear is childish,[41] and it is sentimentalized sufficiently to remain consistent with the opening lines, in which the poet has identified himself as no wise father, but a child; but the fear is also real, with a thin overtone of malice. This opening paragraph preludes the rest of the poem, where both the fear and the attraction of less-than-human life increase.

There are several kinds of incremental development. The next "scene" portrays animals—a cat and some birds—rather than plants. With the growth of various conflicts, such as that between innocence and disillusion, or brute life and human reason, the visualization also becomes more intense; here, Landor assumes a playful equality not with a child, but with the cat. The playful surface controls and in a way also emphasizes the power of deep, resisted emotions which gradually emerge. The poem's resolution is prepared for by hints and contradictions, slowly revealing Landor's response to certain matters: the painful necessity of world-wisdom; separation from

41. Despite (or because of?) what must be called a castration motif.

his boy; separation from the boy's innocence and his own; and a rather ominous, rapt scrutiny of nature.

In the matter of diction, if we accept the "thou" of the first line as a familiar usage, we have granted Landor a flexible medium which will suit his subject while avoiding the baby-talk of "We Are Seven." The latinate descriptive words throughout indicate (like the later "Poeta" and "Pan's Pipe") another aspect of Landor's problem: as a learned man, a poet, he must always have a partly ironic relationship with these children, animals, and plants which he loves and describes so well. Aside from this overtone (which is more explicit in "And reasoned with him on his bloody mind"), Landor's Latin words also give a fine picture of the cat:

> *Does Cincirillo follow thee about?*
> *Inverting one swart foot suspensively,*
> *And waggling his dread jaw, at every chirp*
> *Of bird above him on the olive-branch?*
> *Frighten him then away! 'twas he who slew*
> *Our pigeons, our white pigeons, peacock-tailed,*
> *That fear'd not you and me . . . alas, nor him!*
> *I flattened his striped sides along my knee,*
> *And reasoned with him on his bloody mind,*
> *Till he looked blandly, and half-closed his eyes*
> *To ponder on my lecture in the shade.*

That is: nature is cruel in human moral terms — and has no moral terms, or any terms, of its own, although one may for fun pretend otherwise.

The recognition of the cat's violence is like the vision of Carlino's imagined destructiveness, but the boy's concentration upon the flowers was colored by shame, advancing knowledge, while the cat knows only to remain intent upon every chirp, or rapt in the warm pressure at his side. To lose the cat's "blandness" is the price of wisdom, which human beings must pay:

> *I doubt his memory much, his heart a little,*
> *And in some minor matters (may I say it?)*
> *Could wish him rather sager. But from thee*
> *God hold back wisdom yet for many years!*

Whether in early season or in late
It always comes high priced. For thy pure breast
I have no lesson; it for me has many.

As "(may I say it?)" indicates, the poet, endeavoring to retrieve the pleasures of innocence, or being at home, and of boyhood, assumes as a wistful, self-conscious, and comical game the terms of a more "natural," less conscious being. But the terms are only assumed ironically, and the apparently anti-intellectual sentence ending "it for me has many" also has its double meaning: "I can learn by considering you, as I do by considering Cincirillo, but you cannot learn from watching me — any more than Cincirillo could. You are less happy than he is, but better off than I am; eventually, inevitably, you will become aware of evil, less happy, more adult, more human, and wiser" — as the next vignette shows.

This next passage is the most complete and cruel destruction of the sentimental myth. The idyll of the flowers, the idyll of the child, and the idyll of the animals have all been destroyed by a touch of unpleasant fact. All have been colored by a sense of nature's amoral, attractive beauty; now this sense heightens, and the idyll of the peasants is destroyed by the plainest and most droll fact of all. The statement "For thy pure breast I have no lesson" takes on, by being immediately contradicted, the ironic tone which "a wiser father" would give to the poem's opening line — the tone of an adult speaking to an inferior who will not pay heed. The peasants gyp Carlino:

> *it for me has many.*
> *Come, throw it open then! What sports, what cares*
> *(Since there are none too young for these) engage*
> *Thy busy thoughts? Are you again at work,*
> *Walter and you, with those sly labourers,*
> *Geppo, Giovanni, Cecco and Poeta,*
> *To build more solidly your broken dam*
> *Among the poplars, whence the nightingale*
> *Inquisitively watched you all day long?*
> *I was not of your council in the scheme,*
> *Or might have saved you silver without end,*
> *And sighs too without number.*

Landor has been trying to create a Romantic pastoral in which to lose himself, we might say, and has been failing, since he has a tough knowledge that no one is too young for cares. Childhood is a crumbling dam against punishing, but enlightening experience, and just as nature presents either its own amoral face or a reflection of human guilts and passions, childhood presents either callous ignorance or a reflection of adult pain. The poem is about the poet himself — about his failure, through too much knowledge of nature and childhood, to lose himself in them. The boy would have been better off if his pure breast *could* have learned from his father; the poet would be more at ease if he could recapture a boy's innocence. Sadly, experience gives bitter knowledge when we want retreat, and that process cannot be avoided or replaced.

The distance cannot be closed by revery: the separation in time, miles, and condition of knowledge between boyhood and manhood is insuperable, as is the separation between the human and the non-human. Landor cannot find escape by contemplating innocent, brute nature; as the series of disrupted idylls demonstrates, he finds instead only a deepening of the lessons of experience. The final plaint, the poem's most beautiful passage, constitutes the final idyll of purely sensory experience, of minute details obsessively considered. The frustrated desire to lessen oneself, to become smaller, is repudiated at the same time that it reaches its most outright, extreme statement. As we near the three vital allusions of the closing lines, the wistfully ironic pose of innocence falls increasingly away; similarly, the father who has been speaking to himself drops from his voice the pretence that he can share the smaller, sweeter world. He has, with protest, surrendered to distance.

He uses this full, adult voice, free of irony or mock-simplicity, to define the hopeless temptation of retreat toward a life in which the lush, sensuous particular is all:

> *Art thou gone*
> *Below the mulberry, where that cold pool*
> *Urged to devise a warmer, and more fit*

For mighty swimmers, swimming three abreast?
Or art thou panting in this summer noon
Upon the lowest step before the hall,
Drawing a slice of watermelon, long
As Cupid's bow, athwart thy wetted lips
(Like one who plays Pan's pipe) and letting drop
The sable seeds from all their separate cells,
And leaving bays profound and rocks abrupt,
Redder than coral round Calypso's cave?

Calypso: whose name means "the hider"; who promised unending youth; and who as the *Odyssey* opens has imprisoned the homeward traveler for eight years amid pastoral, sensual pleasures intended to distract him from home and responsibilities. She also calls to mind the other goddess who entertained him — and who changed men into beasts.

The distance of the speaker from the vivid, weirdly concentrated final detail heightens its poignancy. The poem's pattern is one of temptation, of rejected idylls, and futile retreats (like that to the cold pool); as a result, the rapidly focused image also yields a dizzying effect of envelopment and a hint of derangement narrowly escaped. The all-but-microscopic visual experience is magnified to bays, caves, and rocks; the kind and magnitude of the temptation is embodied in this combination of the heroically large with the almost insanely minute. The world of a boy, or that of insensate nature, is so attractive because it is so seductively little, promising to replace the weary pains of intelligence with the protean, finite life of the senses.

Landor was no more influenced by modern anthropology in his choice of Calypso than he was influenced by Freud in his use of "sworded tuberoses" and the "broken hilt." But it is nevertheless interesting to read Joseph Campbell in *The Masks of God* on Calypso:

> In India the power of the goddess-mother finally prevailed to such a degree that the principle of masculine ego initiative was suppressed, even to the point of dissolving the will to individual life; whereas in Greece the masculine will and ego not only held their own, but prospered in a manner that at that time was unique in the world: not in the way of the compulsive

"I want" of childhood (which is the manner and concept of ego normal to the Orient) but in the way of a self-responsible intelligence . . . rationally regarding and responsibly judging the world of empirical fact. . . . And so we come to the journey home, the return of Odysseus from the Underworld and the Island of the Sun . . . cast upon the beaches of the isle of Ogygia, of Calypso of the braided tresses. And the lovely goddess, dwelling there in a cave amid soft meadows, flowers, vines, and birds, singing with a sweet voice while faring to and fro before her loom, weaving with a shuttle, restored him. He dwelt with her eight years (an octave, an eon), assimilating the lessons learned of the first nymph, Circe of the braided tresses. And when the time came, at last, for his departure, Zeus sent the guiding god Hermes [in this context, for Campbell, active self-responsible intelligence] to bid her speed her initiate on his way; which she did, reluctantly.[42]

To read this passage suggests some of the overtones of "Calypso's cave," and tends to give Campbell's theories the blessing of Landor's powerful literary sensibility. Anthropology may be of use to criticism as a substitute for great learning, such as Landor's was. All that he needed to create his image was genius, a sense of "coral cave" as a perfect image of dark retreat amid visual splendor, and his scholarly intimacy with the story of the goddess in her inhumanly beautiful, vine-hung cave, bounded by birds and running water. There, she first tempted the hero with exquisite food, the fabulous locale, her bed, and a promise of — unending youth.

Associated with the frustration of each idyll within the poem is a certain amount of regret and a certain amount of moral agreement; Calypso's fruit-clustered cave and her promise of ageless youth emphasize by their richness, and by Odysseus' rejection of them, the power of his mortal responsibilities. This final scene, like the preceding ones in the poet's Odyssey, is imaginary. To know this, to know that the intense visualization is part of a question, furthers the conflicting emotions of visual grasp and rational loss. The scene's blank verse, beginning with

42. Joseph Campbell, *The Masks of God: Occidental Mythology* (London: Secker and Warburg, 1965), pp. 173–74.

the words "Art thou gone," rises from the more relaxed surface
of the preceding lines in a loftier, tighter measure. The dis-
illusioned fondness of the passages before has verged on loose-
ness of rhythm, a tendency which reaches its climax in a dip
toward prose rhythm; this rhythmic effect poignantly marks the
final capitulation to harsh good sense:

$$I\ was/not\ of/your\ coun/cil\ in/\ the\ scheme. \ldots$$

The forty-four lines preceding this one are so varied in other
ways that one does not notice the fact, but aside from initial
trochees they have been completely iambic, without substitution. The only exception occurs at a similar moment, the close
of the prelude-scene, and even there the one trochee (fourth
position) occurs after a pronounced caesura:

$$Lift\ up\ their\ heads\ at\ once\ \ldots\ not\ with/out\ fear$$
$$That\ they/were\ look/ing\ at/thee\ all/the\ while?$$

Here, in "I was not of your council," the second-position substitution follows an initial one, and after one "straight" iambic
line to restore the measure, the substitution is echoed, joining
two accented syllables with an effect which I find very moving,
and introducing the more electric verse of the close:

$$And\ sighs/too\ with/out\ num/ber.\ Art/thou\ gone. \ldots$$

The closing scene proceeds to outline the temptation in its
most powerful, impregnable form, and in a fuller voice free
now from wistful indulgence, cleaned of pretended innocence.
The two allusions which precede Calypso also mark that the
poet is now of his own counsel, seeing his heartsickness for what
it is, a desire to retreat away from manhood toward what is
finite, simple, and pastoral. When Cupid, the boy about whom
poets traditionally complain, strikes with his bow, it is the next
person *seen* that captures and fascinates the helpless victim,
and Pan's woodland music also is associated with retirement
from the harsh, active life of men. On the other hand, bow and

pipe, images of desire as well as of sensual retirement, are both associated with kinds of poetry, as is Calypso; the references, that is, are in themselves talismans of a learned, unboyish pursuit.

A rhetorical starting point, the conventional Exile's Complaint, grows into a symbolic resignation to several kinds of bitter exile. The occasion of Landor's own actual exile also becomes a rhetorical means, a way to examine the adult poet's distance from several kinds of "home," including Italy, boyhood, innocence, and even his own nostalgia, his concentrated, master's attention to the evidence of the senses. There is no insistence that the experience is unique; apparently, in fact, the poem was deliberately written so as to fit Boccaccio's Italy as well as Landor's. Yet the final statement is incontestably original. In diction, the poem is openly literary, but in a way which allows at least two effective allusions to speech idiom. ("Son, what are you doing," and "I can't teach you anything" both appear in non-realistic "translation" — into the sort of non-imitative language which would *not* lose by translation into a foreign tongue, or by the passage of several hundred years.) The diction further uses its literary language as a means toward flexibility of tone and subject, as when a classical allusion, characteristically, is mingled with a close description of a probably dusty boy eating a slice of watermelon on a very hot day.

In judging such poetry in regard to the criterion of "discovery," one must keep in mind the endeavor to revitalize a cliché by charging the old theme with a hard vein of conscious, unsentimental apprehension. Pound's dictum "make it new" presupposes and even emphasizes an "it." The comparison which "To My Child Carlino" may fairly be expected to bear is with Wordsworth's poems of childhood, in which the fictive illusion is of the poet discovering universal common truths from a situation rather than through conventional procedures. The ideas in these poems are obviously similar to those of "To My Child Carlino," as in Wordsworth's poem "To H. C., Six Years Old":

O blessed vision! happy child!
Thou art so exquisitely wild,
I think of thee with many fears
For what may be thy lot in future years.
  I thought of times when Pain might be thy guest,
Lord of thy house and hospitality;
And Grief, uneasy lover! never rest
But when she sate within the touch of thee.
. . . .

Thou art a dew-drop, which the morn brings forth,
Ill fitted to sustain unkindly shocks,
Or to be trailed along the soiling earth. . . .

A still better known poem is even more relevant; although every
line is to the point, I select a few passages to emphasize as much
as possible the difference from Landor's tone:

Heaven lies about us in our infancy!
Shades of the prison-house begin to close
    Upon the growing boy,
But He beholds the light, and whence it flows,
    He sees it in his joy;
The Youth, who daily farther from the east
    Must travel, still is Nature's Priest,
    And by the vision splendid
    Is on his way attended;
At length the Man perceives it die away,
And fade into the light of common day
. . . .

Behold the Child among his new-born blisses,
A six year's Darling of a pigmy size!
See, where 'mid work of his own hand he lies,
Fretted by sallies of his mother's kisses,
With light upon him from his father's eyes!
. . . .

    Then will he fit his tongue
To dialogues of business, love, or strife;
    But it will not be long
    Ere this be thrown aside,
    And with new joy and pride
The little Actor cons another part;
Filling from time to time his "humorous stage"

> *With all the Persons, down to palsied Age,*
> *That life brings with her in her equipage;*
>   *As if his whole vocation*
>   *Were endless imitation.*

. . . .

>   *Mighty Prophet! Seer blest!*
>   *On whom these truths do rest,*
> *Which we are toiling all our lives to find,*
> *In darkness lost, the darkness of the grave;*
> *Thou over whom thy Immortality*
> *Broods like the Day, a Master o'er a Slave. . . .*

Finally, there is "The Affliction of Margaret" (I take all three
poems from W. H. Auden's selections in his five-volume *Poets
of the English Language*), which coincidentally opens with a
line similar to Landor's:

> *Where art thou, my beloved Son,*
> *Where art thou, worse to me than dead?*

. . . .

> *Ah! Little doth the young-one dream,*
> *When full of play and childish cares,*
> *What power is in his wildest screams,*
> *Heard by his mother unawares!*
> *He knows it not, he cannot guess. . . .*

I do not quote these poems merely to demonstrate the sentiments which every sophomore knows are basic to the thought
of Wordsworth. On the contrary, because "To My Child Carlino" inevitably calls these poems to mind, I quote from them
to say that the ideas are indeed very familiar, and that Landor,
by qualifying them within a thoughtful, complex tonal balance,
tells us more about what it means to say and feel that a boy is
more happy than a man, and closer to nature.

I think that Landor's poem, however I consider the question,
is a better poem than any of the other three. Without attempting to argue this conviction in detail, I hope that I have suggested at least its grounds: Landor's stylistic control achieves
greater depth and complexity of feeling. I find this to be another

way of saying that Landor's poem is more credibly, and with less obstruction, the statement of a particular serious mind.

"To My Child Carlino" carefully makes distinct a certain man's tone of voice as he considers certain thoughts and passions. Wordsworth's poems are less definitions and more openly persuasions, attempts to convince us of the importance, universality, or magnificence of certain thoughts. This project of aggrandizement may establish bardic excitement at the same time as it diminishes definition of the man writing and how he feels; my consciousness of the poems is dominated by Pain-the-guest, dew-drops, prison-houses, Priests, Actors, Pigmies, Prophets, Masters-and-Slaves, short lines, tropes, hyperboles, dramatic "personae," analogies, personifications, and Cowleyan rhymes. Wordsworth, partly because his poems have the intended air of *being* the process of invention, uses a large repertoire of devices for amplification, rather than development, of the subject. That is, the rhetoric of discovery sets itself an additional task, one which is obviated by the rhetoric of conventional statement. This additional task of appearing-to-discover may often proliferate words, tropes, and dramatic devices. Such an element, literary in the pejorative sense, can preclude some of the finer distinctions in the personal attitude of the poet toward his subject. Landor, claiming to make nothing other than a conventional statement, is more free to speak in his own voice as a sensitive, rational, and educated man.

So, Wordsworth and Landor probably had very similar ideas about childhood, but Wordsworth, pursuing certain effects — of "the philosophical," of "the original," etc. — often says some very silly things, or things which will continue to sound silly until one has read a great deal of literary criticism. Pursuing fewer such effects, "To My Child Carlino" arrives at a statement which is similar, but more comprehensible — which is to say, I think, more moving. Beginning with conventional language and procedures, it discovers, in emotional detail, an attitude toward the particular experience which is not "Romanticism"; rather, although the poem may exemplify Romantic preoccupations, it is manifestly what a man might once at the height of his powers have felt. May the reader who treasures the *Ode* at least grant Landor another sort of discovery.

On Music

Many love music but for music's sake,
Many because her touches can awake
Thoughts that repose within the breast half-dead,
And rise to follow where she loves to lead.
What various feelings come from days gone by!
What tears from far-off sources dim the eye!
Few, when light fingers with sweet voices play
And melodies swell, pause, and melt away,
Mind how at every touch, at every tone,
A spark of life hath glisten'd and hath gone.

To My Child Carlino

Carlino! what art thou about, my boy?
Often I ask that question, though in vain;
For we are far apart: ah! therefore 'tis
I often ask it, not in such a tone
As wiser fathers do, who know too well.
Were we not children, you and I together?
Stole we not glances from each other's eyes?
Swore we not secrecy in such misdeeds?
Well could we trust each other. Tell me, then,
What thou art doing. Carving out thy name,
Or haply mine, upon my favourite seat,
With the new knife I sent thee over-sea?
Or hast thou broken it, and hid the hilt
Among the myrtles, starr'd with flowers, behind?
Or under that high throne whence fifty lilies
(With sworded tuberoses dense around)
Lift up their heads at once . . . not without fear
That they were looking at thee all the while?
Does Cincirillo follow thee about?
Inverting one swart foot suspensively,
And wagging his dread jaw, at every chirp
Of bird above him on the olive-branch?
Frighten him then away! 'twas he who slew
Our pigeons, our white pigeons, peacock-tailed,
That fear'd not you and me . . . alas, nor him!
I flattened his striped sides along my knee,

And reasoned with him on his bloody mind,
Till he looked blandly, and half-closed his eyes
To ponder on my lecture in the shade.
I doubt his memory much, his heart a little,
And in some minor matters (may I say it?)
Could wish him rather sager. But from thee
God hold back wisdom yet for many years!
Whether in early season or in late
It always comes high priced. For thy pure breast
I have no lesson; it for me has many.
Come, throw it open then! What sports, what cares
(Since there are none too young for these) engage
Thy busy thoughts? Are you again at work,
Walter and you, with those sly labourers,
Geppo, Giovanni, Cecco, and Poeta,
To build more solidly your broken dam
Among the poplars, whence the nightingale
Inquisitively watched you all day long?
I was not of your council in the scheme,
Or might have saved you silver without end,
And sighs too without number. Art thou gone
Below the mulberry, where that cold pool
Urged to devise a warmer, and more fit
For mighty swimmers, swimming three abreast?
Or art thou panting in this summer noon
Upon the lowest step before the hall,
Drawing a slice of watermelon, long
As Cupid's bow, athwart thy wetted lips
(Like one who plays Pan's pipe) and letting drop
The sable seeds from all their separate cells,
And leaving bays profound and rocks abrupt,
Redder than coral round Calypso's cave?

"Ye Who Have Toil'd":
The Theme of the Past

All correct perceptions are the effect of careful practice.

The Pentameron (Works, *9:162*

Poems about Recalling the Past

In Landor's well-known epigram,

> *Borgia, thou once wert almost too august,*
> *And high for adoration; — now thou'rt dust!*
> *All that remains of thee these plaits unfold —*
> *Calm hair, meand'ring with pellucid gold!*

the justly celebrated graces of writing, I have suggested, express certain themes which persist in Landor's work: a concern with time, in relation to history and in relation to personal mortality; the opposing ideas of serenity and transiency; and, giving a special direction to these traditional themes, Landor's intense but rather pessimistic passion to restore that which is lost in time.

A textual variant (which may or may not reflect a revision) aptly symbolizes the conflicts in Landor's pessimism. When the poem was first published, the last word in the third line above read "infold"; the changed letter marks the difference between the calm hair revealing what little remains, or imprisoning it.

The quibble is interesting as a footnote to certain other poems. One of the finest of these might be said to violate Landor's disapproval of allegory:

> *Ye who have toil'd uphill to reach the haunt*
> *Of other men who lived in other days,*
> *Whether the ruins of a citadel*
> *Rais'd on the summit by Pelasgic hands,*
> *Or chamber of the distaff and the song . . .*
> *Ye will not tell what treasure there ye found,*
> *But I will.*
>   *Ye found there the viper laid*
> *Full-length, flat-headed, on a sunny slab,*
> *Nor loth to hiss at ye while crawling down.*
> *Ye saw the owl flap the loose ivy leaves*
> *And, hooting, shake the berries on your heads.*
>   *Now, was it worth your while to mount so high*
> *Merely to say ye did it, and to ask*
> *If those about ye ever did the like?*
> *Believe me, O my friends, 'twere better far*
> *To stretch your limbs along the level sand*
> *As they do, where small children scoop the drift,*
> *Thinking it must be gold, where curlews soar*
> *And scales drop glistening from the prey above.*

I find the poem's tone strangely affecting.[1] This quality of strangeness I trace, finally, to the bitter, strong emotion conveyed by a subject which one might expect to classify as cool and intellectual. But definition of that subject calls for the risk of paraphrase.

First, who is meant by "ye"? The poem is addressed to those who, like Landor, have struggled to attain, by study or by the discipline of verse, an intellectual comprehension of the past. This endeavor of the spirit, for Landor, includes all efforts of the mind toward civilization, poetry constituting the highest of these; the goal is not necessarily to write about the ancients, or to write as they did — rather, the goal is "to reach the haunt," to write and think with a perfect understanding of what they

1. "Ye Who Have Toil'd" was published in 1863, four years after the poems of Landor's supposed senility (see p. 143 below).

understood. The great rough-cut Pelasgic stones are the oldest form of masonry found in modern Greece; they constitute nearly all that we know of the Pelasgians, for they inhabited Greece before the Hellenes. Their ruins were old, and hence inscrutable, even in antiquity. The ruins and the chamber can represent two kinds of ancient experience — heroic versus lyrical,[2] practical versus artistic — as well as the past-embracing "toils" of history and poetry.

"Ye" thus denotes people who are similar to Landor; but as the poem's conclusion shows, they are also not Landor, and not all of the contempt is self-addressed. Perhaps it is better to say that he is of their number, and that some of them are distinct from him. At any rate, the sudden idiomatic turn of lines 6 and 7, interrupts, with the aplomb of direct syntax, the gush of a blowsily grand period. A heavy midfoot caesura and the lilting stress upon "I" contribute to the same effect, which will be repeated with "Now, was it worth your while. . . ."

Many of us, then, who endeavor to become the peers and inheritors of past civilization, do not realistically confess the true nature of our rewards, once we have made the climb — "but I will." The poem now introduces the crisp images which, especially in the final lines, strike counter to the apparently bardic mode of other lines. Of course, "haunt," "who lived in other days," "summit," "chamber," and " 'twere better far" are only superficially loose and overblown. These expectedly "poetic" phrases are precise in context, and they also serve an ironic function. They represent one of two voices: Landor speaks first with the rounded, almost persuasive voice of one confident in the great success of "reaching" culture.[3] This rhetorical voice is

2. See "Ode To A Friend," stanza IX:

> *'Tis not Pelasgic wall,*
> *By him made sacred, whom alone*
> *'Twere not profane to call*
> *The Bard Divine nor (thrown*
> *Far under me) Valdarno, nor the crest*
> *Of Vallombrosa in the purple east.*

3. As a master of rhythm, Landor is very adept at undercutting, to fine degrees, the swell of convincing rhetoric. This technique can, as in the

countered by the tone of one who is bitingly aware that the past always remains to some measure resistant; the second, more pessimistic tone replaces the grandly general figures of the chamber, distaff, and citadel — which were impressive in their way — with harder, more closely animated images. The second of the poem's two paragraphs renders an actual place, abruptly turning the ascent from a mere figurative vehicle into a vivid scene, one which nearly obscures the tenor. The tenor, "to reach the spirit of the past," had seemed almost tritely clear.

Those who by arts of prose, verse, or study confront the past, and so do become to some extent the heirs of history, are loath to admit their true rewards. Their "treasure" is represented by a frightening encounter with non-human nature. The jungle, opposite of what "ye" sought, is unfriendly. The encounter is comic as well as brutal, but the principle effect produced by the

---

opening lines of "Ye Who Have Toil'd," maintain the convincing roll in most of its effect while qualifying it with a very small measure of irony; that is one end of the spectrum. The technique may be traced from the other end by beginning with the parody of Byron's "We sat down and wept by the waters," and other burlesques, proceeding to the somewhat slower curve of:

> *The mermaid sat upon the rocks*
> > *All day long,*
> *Admiring her beauty and combing her locks,*
> > *And singing a mermaid song.*
>
> *And hear the mermaid's song you may,*
> > *As sure as you can be,*
> *If you will but follow the sun all day*
> > *And souse with him into the sea.*

The fun of that poem, produced by Shakespeare in Landor's "Citation and Examination of William Shakespeare" is largely in the rhythm; so is the effect of the following poem, with its fine proportion of deflating wit (again the occasion is dramatic, for the Emperor quotes the poem as his father's in "Emperor of China and Tsing-Ti"):

> *The narrow mind is the discontented one.*
> *There is pleasure in wisdom, there is wisdom in pleasure.*
> *If thou findest no honey in thy cake,*
> *Put thy cake into honey with thine own right-hand,*
> *Nor think it defiled thereby.*

The Epicureanism is not offensively smug because it is presented archly. The free-verse rhythm of these lines, half muttered and half shouted, provides a useful substitute for what Mark Twain called "swearing."

animals, who have repossessed the scene of past order, is one of
fear and discomfort. In what remains of the past, we find not a
philosophic, antiquarian calm, but devastation, the threat of
danger, and grotesque, irrational fear. I think that a proper
paraphrase of owl and viper should include several references:
the violent and incomprehensibly alien elements in the past
itself; that natural decay of fact which is our own ignorance;
the ignorance of contemporaries (pedantic dons and yahoo
critics?) who do not honor even the minimal achievement of
reaching the ruin; and the imagined indignation of the classical intelligences whom the climbers would ape.

All of these meanings can be included by saying that the hostile, ominous "treasure" represents a special variety of loss, a
loss too frightening, too objective, and too direly felt to be
called merely "ignorance," although it is akin to ignorance. The
viper and owl are the real, unsympathetic detritus with which
time replaces the decayed human forms of civilization. They are
the living, brute facts which replace the past, intervening between the climber and his goal, between Landor and heroic
Greece. They are also, I think, the presence of something savage,
mutable, and resistant in heroic Greece itself. The past too
has its ocean of contingency, and since all irrelevance is equal
and familiar, it is this part of the past which the climber is
most likely to encounter. The treasure reflects very pessimistically upon the toil. With the third paragraph, this pessimism
appears to be extended: the descriptive rhetoric of the grotesque
encounter is interrupted by a dry idiom similar to the "But I
will" that deflated another kind of rhetorical passage:

> *Now, was it worth your while to mount so high*
> *Merely to say ye did it, and to ask*
> *If those about ye ever did the like?*

The lines apply perfectly to the vehicle, the climbing-scene. And
they have an apparently devastating effect as reinforcement of
the mockery on another level: since to "reach" the classical
temper (or a fact of history, or the art of verse) is unappreciated,
and probably a hollow delusion in itself — since in such pur-

suits you gain only the discomfort which stems from heightened perception (of serpentine evil, or of your own timid folly), what good is your earnest seeking?

The answer is, no good, unless the prescription of the next lines is ironic, as I believe it is; or, it is ironic except as applied to those who do pursue their art merely to say that they did it, merely to claim the powers of a learned mind as one would claim a difficult slope. The poet has twice promised us plain talk; once, to describe how unrewarding, in relation to personal gain or comfort, the heights can be, and now again, to say how much pleasanter it is to linger on the sea-level plain, attempting little. And indeed, without irony, it *would* be "better far." Landor qualifies this preference as to personal good in a characteristic manner, with a strikingly concentrated visual detail.

It is personally better and easier if one can join "those about ye," prone, passive, and on a single level; there, children are pleased by the drift, happily deluded that it is solid and of intrinsic worth. These images of mediocrity, comfort, and childish delusion all direct the eye downward. All, like the viper and the owl, are seen by those within the poem; that is, the climbers, as well as the poet, could see the animals, just as now "those about ye" feel the sand, and the children, as well as the poet, can see and touch the attractive, insubstantial foam. But in the final, eighteenth and nineteenth lines.

> *where curlews soar*
> *And scales drop glistening from the prey above.*

the image is asserted by "I", the poet. "Ye" may or may not see the curlew or the tiny motes of downdrifting light. They are there, and they direct the eye irresistibly upward — back, in other words, toward the ominous, hypnotically attractive realm of endeavor. That single gesture, of looking upward toward a scene of violent, hard-to-perceive beauty, contradicts the pessimistic prescription to stretch out and enjoy personal comfort. It is "better far" to be one of the crowd on the level and to mistake the drift for gold, but for the speaker (and for his true peers or "friends"), the magical, downfiltering lure of the heights cannot be withstood.

The final judgment is, very approximately: "this endeavor is not, as those pretend who achieve only its superficial goals, an easy matter, or even one which leads to any measurable attainment, or much attainment of any kind beyond itself. Rather, it is disturbing and difficult work; far from comfortable, it sharpens and emphasizes one's fears, one's perception of evil, and one's frustrating perception of loss, the accumulation of time."

The fusion of an elusive, ominous, yet attractive "nature" with a "history" of similar qualities is characteristic and compelling. The same can be said of the fresh imagery used in conjunction with conventional language, and of the very concentrated final image which is made to bear maximum weight by such strategies as concluding on the word "above." The abrupt focus on floating spots of light epitomizes, in itself, the kind of alert mastery in which one must deal; rather than confident, hollow command of a body of fact or technique ("merely to say ye did it"), the poet chooses to transfix the violent, mysterious, and barely evident moment. He will not write an all-inclusive biography of Pericles, leaving his partial mastery of the intervening centuries to be assumed by the reader; rather, the reader may assume that Landor has touched the scholarly summit, seeing and judging the mastery of spirit in Landor's avowedly fictional accounts of the unknown Pericles, his conversations and poems. Juxtaposing imagined, glistening particulars with known, factual generalities, Landor's characteristic forms in prose and verse constitute an ironic, modest critique of his own life's ambitions.

But the most important aspect of "Ye Who Have Toil'd" is the passion with which he treats his subject, so that the subject's only adequate definition is the poem. The underlying seriousness of the irony, the harsh intensity of the flat-headed snake and the limbs stretched along the level sand, announce that Landor is not merely talking about "learning" — or, if he is, then we must understand learning in the broadest and deepest sense we can, to include nearly all of the redeeming qualities of the mind. He is pessimistic about knowing the past, but he also knows that it is the past in which we live.

The theme, in many permutations, was lifelong. In *Gebir*, written when he was in his early twenties and well over fifty years before "Ye Who Have Toil'd," the snake first appears. *Gebir*, a remarkable poem though fragmented in subject, is ostensibly about the futility and eventual doom of invasion and colonization, and it is indeed usually read as a political allegory, in accordance with the "moral" Landor offered after the poem had been attacked as obscure.[4] But the selfless hero, Gebir, is very far from being an overweening tyrant,[5] and the submerged theme of the poem is the futility and eventual doom of attempts to restore or to fulfill the past.[6] Gebir, the young ruler of Boetic Spain, has invaded Egypt in obedience to a childhood oath; there his ancestor Sidad once founded a city, which Gebir resolves to excavate and restore. His army begins the bad-fated work as Book II opens; the viper's appearance is the climax of this scene, which deserves fairly full quotation:

> *The Gadite men the royal charge obey.*
> *Now fragments, weigh'd up from th' uneven streets,*
> *Leave the ground black beneath; again the sun*
> *Shines into what were porches, and on steps*
> *Once warm with frequentation — clients, friends,*

4. See Landor's preface, *The Complete Works of Walter Savage Landor*, ed. T. Earle Welby and Stephen Wheeler, 16 vols. (London; Chapman and Hall Ltd., 1927–36), 13:344.

5. Gebir, the invader, is in fact rather an ideal ruler (unlike his ancestors); for example, see Book II, lines 89–90:

> *My heart, indeed, is full: but witness, heaven!*
> *My people, not my passion, fills my heart.*

6. Thus, *Gebir* may represent Landor's most personal treatment of the Prometheus figure, a theme to which he returned many times. De Quincey considered *Count Julian* superior not only to Shelley's Prometheus, but to any such figure "since Milton's Satan." *Count Julian* was in fact "the most fearful lesson extant of the great moral that crime propagates crime and violence inherits violence." ("Notes on W. S. Landor," *Tait's Edinburgh Magazine*, 14(1847):103.)

All morning; satchel'd idlers all mid-day,
Lying half-up, and languid, though at games.
    Some raise the painted pavement, some on wheels
Draw slow its laminous length, some intersperse
Salt waters through the sordid heaps, and sieze
The flowers and figures starting fresh to view.
Others rub hard large masses, and essay
To polish into white what they misdeem
The growing green of many trackless years.[7]

. . . .

Here, arches are discover'd, there, huge beams
Resist the hatchet, but in fresher air
Soon drop away: there spreads a marble, squar'd
And smoothen'd; some high pillar, for its base,
Chose it, which now lies ruin'd in the dust.
Clearing the soil at bottom, they espy
A crevice; they, intent on treasure, strive
Strenuous, and groan, to move it: one exclaims
"I hear the rusty metal grate: it moves!"
Now, overturning it, backward they start;
And stop again, and see a serpent pant,
See his throat thinken, and the crisped scales
Rise ruffled; while upon the middle fold
He keeps his wary head and blinking eye,
Curling more close, and crouching ere he strike.

Obvious features of the passage, such as the ancient slab, the word "treasure," and the climactic near-focus, seem to adumbrate "Ye Who Have Toil'd" quite directly. So too does the misdeeming of verd-antique, confusing patina with substance — a fine detail, if one does not find it a trifle too ingenious, almost to the point of pedantry. But *Gebir*'s impression, as a whole, is one of stylistic powers and discoveries sometimes crammed together and lacking a whole conception adequate to their freshness and power. Like much in the poem, the above lines are interesting for their distance in spirit from the eighteenth century, which in fact had a few years to run when they were composed. Nevertheless, despite the intrusion of unmalleable political enthusiasms and the distraction of sheer stylistic exu-

7. Landor's note: "The *Verde Antico* [a kind of marble] is of this country."

berance, *Gebir* does achieve a compact narrative unity relatively unusual in narrative poetry of its kind and place. Much of this unity (consistency or coherence might be a better term) rests upon the theme of Gebir as the man who struggles actively to manage the impossible: to overcome time, to penetrate the past. His career is contrasted with a pastoral subplot which tells the story of his brother, Tamar, a shepherd.

Tamar wrestles with a nymph and loses; then after Gebir defeats her on Tamar's behalf, Tamar marries her and they leave on an idyllic voyage. The ceremony and journey complete the subplot and comprise the beautifully written Book VI. In the course of the journey she gives Tamar a vision of their descendants, who will be just rulers — a matter which had never occurred to unambitious Tamar. At the close of Book VI they have a vision of beneficent, personified Time eventually bringing future men wisdom, justice, "and glory that shall strike the crystal stars" (final line, Book VI).

In contrast, Gebir struggles to restore his city, and fails. He defeats Tamar's nymph, but dies before his own marriage with Charoba can take place. His journey is to the underworld, where he meets his extremely unpleasant forebears (a thinly disguised George III among them), and where he learns from his father that the ancestral oath, whose keeping causes Gebir's downfall, was a sinful, vindictive error. Gebir soon dies, with his just ambitions and his marriage both cut off. Parallel to the glorious close of Tamar's journey, Gebir's journey to Hell (Book III) ends with Gebir's anguished, unanswered questioning of mortality; as he asks his question,

> all his strength dissolved
> *Within him, thunder shook his troubled brain;*
> *He started; and the cavern's mouth survey'd*
> *Near; and beyond, his people; he arose,*
> *And bent towards them his bewilder'd way.*

This is the conclusion of Book III, which began with a prologue-passage. There the poet complains that he cannot, lacking Shakespeare's supernatural power, resurrect dead men and ages by poetic art. Can anyone do so? "Rather, can any, with out-stripping voice," the prologue closes, "The parting Sun's gigantic strides recall?" "The parting Sun" is not (as at first appears) Shakespeare, but passing time, and the lines finally doubt whether "any man" at all can perfectly recreate what has been. Landor's own footnote glosses those lines:

> "Can any man bring back the far-off intercepted hills," or can I hope to "lead up long-absent heroes into day," so as to exhibit their perfect character by a just description of their actions?

A few dozen lines farther on, a variation of this statement is pronounced by the shade who guides Gebir to the "discontented and deserted shades" of his warlike ancestors, sentenced now "to be enclosed / Within a limit, and that limit fire." These "long-absent heroes" are not resigned to darkness:

> *such penitence,*
> *Such contemplation theirs! Thy ancestors*
> *Bear up against them, nor will they submit*
> *To conquering time th' asperities of Fate.*

The same passage implies comparison of the statesman's desire to live by fame in the future with the poet's complementary desire to bring the past to life by art; both are viewed pessimistically.

Such relationships remain half-realized in *Gebir*'s thematically fragmented, although rich, context. Yet the poem's many directions of meaning do not collapse to mere rhetoric. That Gebir, not Tamar, is the hero, preserves *Gebir* from shallow sentimentality; at the root of this sympathy for the doomed, ambitious venturer into the past are the young poet's own dreads and ambitions.

The ancestral city which Landor would restore is, in effect, tradition: the arts, the heroes, and the spirit of what has been. The problem of conceiving something emotionally near, yet apart from oneself — especially something from which one is parted by time — had also a profound personal meaning for

Landor. This more intimate yearning to embrace a more personal past finds expression in "Memory," a poem of Landor's
old age:

> *The mother of the Muses, we are taught,*
> *Is Memory: she has left me; they remain,*
> *And shake my shoulder, urging me to sing*
> *About the summer days, my loves of old.*
> Alas! Alas! *is all I can reply.*
> *Memory has left with me that name alone,*
> *Harmonious name, which other bards may sing,*
> *But her bright image in my darkest hour*
> *Comes back, in vain comes back, call'd or uncall'd.*
> *Forgotten are the names of visitors*
> *Ready to press my hand but yesterday;*
> *Forgotten are the names of earlier friends*
> *Whose genial converse and glad countenance*
> *Are fresh as ever to mine ear and eye;*
> *To these, when I have written, and besought*
> *Remembrance of me, the word* Dear *alone*
> *Hangs on the upper verge, and waits in vain.*
> *A blessing wert thou, O oblivion,*
> *If thy stream carried only weeds away,*
> *But vernal and autumnal flowers alike*
> *It hurries down to wither on the strand.*

Only Landor could write with such force and distinction about
his blurring, weakening powers, and only his special preoccupations could give such serious, decorous breadth to a poem
apparently "about" senility. As so often, the very personal is dis-
tilled — not extrapolated — into the generic.

"Memory" is not about senility, but about memory, art, and
personal relationship; each of these is imperfect, the poem
confesses, as a means of preserving what is human from the
passing years. Thus, the subject is not only failing memory,
but failing existence; the poet's consciousness is dying gradually. And, because of time's work upon himself as well as upon
his friends, the memory *of him* — which he beseeches — dies
also as men age and die.

Typifying Landor's adroit renewal of conventional figures,
the opening personification makes the statement more complex,

not more conventional: memory is not really the mother of art, for in this context, at least, recall does not precede creation. Rather, the muses foster memory; the alert habits of style waken the man and, at last, his memory.

The exposition of that process is fairly complex. First, the poet is wakened to despair, and then to the memory only of a name — not a real name, but the literary bard-name which he devised for the woman of his love poems. (Landor invented the harmonizing of "Jane" to "Ianthe" and subsequently wrote several poems on the invention and on its adaptation by other poets.) With terror, he for a moment knows only her name, but with a sort of bitter triumph her bright image returns. The emotion is reflected by the movement of this line, which throws still further, before at last concluding, a prolonged sentence whose increasing excitement is the result of repetitions:

>*Comes back, in vain comes back, call'd or uncall'd.*

By halting increments, at first, he overcomes the mind's nightfall to see her clearly, by means of her important role in his art. Ianthe has led him to Jane; the muses have given life to memory. "In vain," though: because Ianthe's presence is intermittent, arising not through will but when the muses shake Landor's shoulder; because she is dead, and because the powers of his art, the habits which can call her image to mind, are no longer strong enough to sing her name.

The poem next begins a nearly trite, though terrible, observation: I remember my long-grieved love better than I remember yesterday's visitors. This statement leads, however, to the grammatically parallel "Forgotten are the names of earlier friends . . . ." These sincerely loved friends are, as memories, in opposite situations from that of the dead lover: the poet recalls their presence, but not their names. Thus, the visitors who come to press the old poet's hand — to mark presence with a token, to say "I know you" — attain a new significance. There are several kinds of remembering and forgetting at stake. These, and a personal dread of extinction, are represented in the poem by civilized artifices. These institutions range from a handshake, to letter writing, to poetry, which is seen in its role as a kind of human relationship.

First the dead woman is recalled through a mere name and through the role of lover-poet which that sobriquet recalls. Almost *as a result* of forgetfulness, because she has become in some measure his creation, because, at least, she has been emblemized by a harmonious name, he recalls her with forcible brightness. She lives partly through having been refined to a nominal token. The living visitors, each of whom existed only in a name or in other social tokens, are forgotten.

Finally, the also-living friends, although remembered and perhaps remembering, have lost in the poet's intelligence that token by which they might still be known, more fully known. This realization and the word *Dear*, hanging on the upper verge of blankness, horrify because that verge presages death not only from the world but from human minds. This latter, most awful death begins even before actual death and continues long after it. Not only do men die; so too do thoughts and feelings. All of our arts are, like social forms, but temporary stays and comforts against an oblivion cold as blank paper.

In a way, the poem could not be more gloomy, for there is nothing optimistic about Ianthe's "bright image" and its return; all of this will end, and is in vain. The slow dissolution of memory is a soft whisper that the self, too, dissolves. This pervasive blackness is relieved, explicitly, only by the definite though doomed reality of Landor's affections: although in vain, because she is dead, Ianthe's image does persist, almost outliving the mind which conceives it.

And, although in vain because human faculties erode, Landor's affection and his desire for communication remain, expressed by the formality of an ironically poignant, solitary word:

> *the word* Dear *alone*
> *Hangs on the upper verge, and waits in vain.*

The past is lost beyond recovery. But its strength is that it has been, and cannot be changed. Although not permanent, the gestures of the mind are real and have reality beyond much that is more immediately present.

Fading memory, then, is made to suggest fading life, the loss necessarily entailed by every large or small passage of time. This disappearance of life into time is suggested by a surface devoted in part to social matters such as letters and visits; carelessly read, the poem might seem to make the opposite statement, might appear to affirm the long durance of the heart's recollections while all else dies. In fact, the statement is that — "alas" — even those diamond-bright recollections are in vain, and must vanish. In "Death of the Day," a fine short poem on a similar theme, aspects of the statement are explicit which were implicit in "Memory," and vice versa. (This poem, incidentally, was written several years *after* "Memory.")

> *Death of the Day*
>
> *My pictures blacken in their frames*
> *As night comes on.*
> *And youthful maids and wrinkled dames*
> *Are now all one.*
>
> *Death of the Day! A sterner Death*
> *Did worse before;*
> *The fairest form, the sweetest breath,*
> *Away he bore.*

"Memory," a poem evidently about memory and aging, implies a further statement about death. This poem, conversely, invests a death lament with a consciousness of the gradual death which comes to mind, body, and person.

This further theme is most apparent if the initial stanza is first considered by itself: as life closes, the poet's awareness of extinction becomes more pervasive, his distinguishing awareness of life diminishes. His memory, his concern, and his perception all grow dull; all women will be the same when they die, and the same to him when he dies. As gradually as dusk, moreover, does this state approach. All of this is set, of course, within an actual room hung with pictures, during an actual dusk. But the scene is not a mere picturesque setting or metaphorical repetition for the second stanza.

Not only is literal, real death more "stern" and absolute than the gradual death of memory and concern. The further horror is that once dead, the particular, mourned woman is also "all one" with the other dead. The dead are all equally young, equally old, equally sweet and fair. The unexpected and even surprising element in the poem's conclusion is what in another poem might be the most obvious element: the poet cares passionately about one particular dead woman. He has constructed the feeling that it all, past and present, is the same to him, implying that individual personalities are "in vain." But now he reveals that he feels deeply — indeed absolutely — about one who is not, to him, "all one" with the rest of the past. That feeling for her is made more pathetic because it is, by the context of the first stanza, in vain. To the passing days, although not to the poet, she is one more woman. He will die, and her stern, actual death will be succeeded by the death, with him, of his feeling for her. The "Day" which dies is the day of his life, of his concern with life, and of her continued memory in his mind. The extreme feeling of the final two lines is balanced by the admission of the first stanza that even the "fairest form" must merge into the anonymous past.

"Memory" proceeded from a recalled image to the pessimistic admission that, for all of its force, feeling must disappear into the numberless years. "Death of the Day" begins by asserting the impartiality of passing time, then adds the temporary presence of a recalled image in one ferociously partial mind. Neither of these very similar poems modifies the recognition of death through any apparent moralization: there is no religious or Romantically quasi-religious affirmation; no carpe-diem turning toward life; no consolation of "ars longa." Instead, both poems are pervaded by what one can call Landor's sentimental stoicism, a detachment which is partly aesthetic — is, partly, the dignified formality of the verse. This aspect of Landor's attitude is embodied in the stately movement of "Death of the Day" in four-syllable units. That difficult norm is maintained without awkwardness or obtrusiveness and is broken only in the first line. Such formal severities temper the extreme feeling so that rather than maudlin it is, finally, nearly the opposite. The external counterpart of this internal, technical restraint is, in both of these poems, the remote, invulnerable quality of the past itself: the quality of Borgia's mysterious, unliving hair.

That is to say, the pessimism of "Memory" is offset only by the brilliant, although vanished, image of a woman whose life has passed: although this did not endure, it was. And the sentence "it was" lends to the given fact — whether remembered, groped after, or even forgotten — a distant, marble aloofness. Similar is the stoicism of maintaining, in the face of twilight, that the worst has already happened; the sterner death has taken Ianthe, and so has removed her, as it will soon remove Landor and his affection for her, beyond time's further menace, into the calm.

The Two Texts of the English Idylls

The special and compelling calm of what is past appears most prominently in Landor's poems about antiquity, notably the *Hellenics* and certain dramatic poems. Before discussing some of those poems, I want to clarify what I have to say about their nature by introducing some biographical evidence and by raising a bibliographical question which in an almost comical way reflects upon the role of memory in Landor's life.

Stephen Wheeler's edition of Landor's poems is, as to accuracy and completeness, highly respectable. Unfortunately, though, the work is awkwardly old-fashioned in several ways: the poems, in uninviting double columns, are arranged in silly categories (such as "Town and Countryside" or "Poems of Love and Friendship") rather than chronologically by publication.

Furthermore, the earliest versions of the poems are printed in the text, with all later variants — even though nearly all of these are authorial revisions — squeezed into the bottom of the page.[8] Using these variants and the original editions, I have chosen to quote Landor's poetry in versions incorporating the latest substantive changes which can be safely assumed to come from Landor's hand.

My one important exception to that procedure is a very important one indeed: the *Hellenics*, which present large, unique problems in criticism, biography, and textual study. Certain of these poems are in two versions. I use the earlier when discussing an entire poem, but my incidental quotations from these poems are (as I then note) from the later version. My reasons for this practice will emerge from an account of the whole problem.

Ten of the *Hellenics* were originally composed in Latin verse as the *Idyllia Heroica*, including "Dryope," "Pan and Pitys," "Cupid and Pan," and others of the most interesting *Hellenics* (a title which Landor first used in his 1846 *Works*). Landor translated these poems and published them in 1847 in a volume entitled *The Hellenics of Walter Savage Landor, Enlarged and Completed* (London: Edward Moxon, 1847). While working on this translation, Landor, then seventy-one years old, surveyed a career of more than fifty years and wrote in a letter: "My Idyls will atone for all my sins against poetry in Tragedies &c &c." [9]

Ten years later, a translation of Landor's "Cupido et Pan" into pentameter couplets by one G. G. Cunningham appeared in the *Gentleman's Magazine* for March, 1857. Cunningham's couplets are not only vastly worse than Landor's English version of 1847, they are, considering that the Latin original is a

8. Geoffrey Grigson's *Poems* presents a very full selection, sensibly arranged, in an attractive volume with some notes and a short introduction. Unfortunately the texts used are not perfectly consistent and reliable. Also, Grigson includes much junk, while omitting poems like "Child of a Day," "On a Hair of Lucrezia Borgia," "My Pictures Blacken in Their Frames," and "On Music." Geoffrey Grigson, *Poems* (Carbondale: Southern Illinois University Press, 1964).

9. R. H. Super, *Walter Savage Landor: A Biography* (New York: New York University Press, 1954), p. 377.

very brilliant poem, inferior to most poems ever written by anyone. Landor's published English version obviously was unknown to Cunningham and to his editor. The amazing thing is that by a double coincidence it was also apparently unknown to Landor. Along with Cunningham's adulatory verses addressed to Landor, "Cupid and Pan" is accompanied in the *Gentleman's* by the following, authentic, "Copy of note addressed to the translator."

> My dear Sir; I had no idea that any man living could translate my Idylls. You have performed the first admirably. Proud shall I be if you continue the task with all the others of them.
>
> I return your proof with a few corrections; a very few, and chiefly in punctuation. I abhor dashes. The verses you do me the honor of addressing to me personally will make me proud for life. I must shew them to the young ladies who patronize a man who entered his 83rd year yesterday.
>
> Very truly yours, W. S. Landor

The best explanation which we have, on the basis of known evidence, is R. H. Super's assumption that Landor in his senility forgot the English versions about which he had been so enthusiastic.[10] But this explanation would be far more satisfying if Landor had now died, or retreated into mumbling inanition, concerning himself with dashes and with the patronizing young ladies, while Cunningham did his wretched best with the nine remaining *Idyllia*.

But Cunningham did not take up the poems; Landor did. Super deduces from letters that "in the latter part of May he was well embarked on the task."[11] In 1859 James Nichol of Edinburgh published *The Hellenics of Walter Savage Landor, Comprising Heroic Idyls, &c, New Edition, Enlarged.* All of the ten *Idyllia* (except *The Last of Ulysses*, which Landor never republished in English) appear in new translations. The old man was no less enthusiastic about his new translations than about those of 1847. In one of the letters whereby the work on

10. *Ibid.*, p. 451. See also R. H. Super, *The Publication of Landor's Works* (London: The Bibliographical Society 1954), p. 40.
11. Super, *Walter Savage Landor*, p. 451.

the new version is dated, the poems which ten years before had been Landor's "atonement" are again very highly valued indeed: "Whoever may read or may not read them, I will take care that the volume shall contain more of good poetry and less of bad or indifferent, than any other since the days of Alfieri." [12] He gives no indication of remembering the poems published a decade earlier.

The poems of 1859 are not senile. They are as different from the 1847 versions as two close translations by the same author can be, but one would be very hard put to decide which group of poems, as a whole, is better. The temptation sometimes is to glean a passage from each and reconstruct a poem containing the maximum number of one's favorite lines. In his *Poems*, Grigson, without a full explanation, prints the 1847 "Cupid and Pan" and the 1859 "Pan and Pitys."

In general, the later poems are shorter, less mannered, and less likely to be awkward or long-winded. They are also somewhat less vigorous. Although of an equally frank and deliberate archaism ("Denyest thou," etc.), they contain fewer grammatical inversions, or inversions which are less prominent, and their descriptive passages are often more condensed.

Such, at least, are my conclusions, but they are very generalized conclusions; the two versions, although independent, take similar, fairly close orbits about their Latin original. It may be convenient to bring the two versions together on the page. Two passages from each version of "Pan and Pitys," chosen more or less at random, illustrate the degree and perhaps the kind of differences. Lines 26–46, 1847:

> *"Thy reed had crackled with thy flames, and split*
> *With torture after torture; thy lament*
> *Had fill'd the hollow rocks; but when it came*
> *To touch the sheep-fold, there it paus'd and cool'd.*
> *Wonderest thou whence the story reached my ear?*
> *Why open those eyes wider? Why assume*
> *The ignorant, the innocent? prepared*
> *For refutation, ready to conceal*

12. *Ibid.*, p. 451.

The fountain of Selinos, waving here
On the low water its long even grass,
And there (thou better may'st remember this)
Paved with smooth stones, as temples are. The sheep
Who led the rest, struggled ere yet half-shorn,
And dragged thee slithering after it: thy knee
Bore long the leaves of ivy twined around
To hide the scar, and still the scar is white.
Dost thou deny the giving half thy flock
To Cynthia? hiding tho' the better half,
Then all begrimed producing it, while stood
Well-washt and fair in puffy wooliness
The baser breed, and caught the unpracticed eye."

Lines 23–44, 1859:

"Ay, thy reeds crackled with thy scorching flames
And burst with sobs and groans . . . the snow-white flock
Was safe, the love-sick swain kept sharp look there.
Wonderest thou such report should reach my ear?
And widenest thou thine eyes, half-ready now
To swear it all away, and to conceal
The fountain of Selinos. So! thou knowest
Nothing about that shallow brook, those herbs
It waves in running, nothing of the stones
Smooth as the pavement of a temple-floor,
And how the headstrong leader of the flock
Broke loose from thy left-hand, and in pursuit
How falledst thou, and how thy knee was bound
With ivy lest white hairs betray the gash.
Denyest thou that by thy own accord
Cynthia should share thy flock and take her choice?
Denyest thou damping and sprinkling o'er
With dust, and shutting up within a cave
Far out of sight, the better breed? the worse
Displayed upon the bank below, well washt,
Their puffy fleeces glittering in the sun.
Shame! To defraud with gifts, and such as these!"

The two passages are sufficiently typical. As a unit, the first
one is probably preferable: because the burning pipe is ex-
ploited in the suavity of concrete metaphor, and not merely
glossed into "sobs and groans"; because the river-plants and the

escaping sheep are conveyed more memorably; and because of a general air of fullness. The "hollow rocks," for example, are an attempt to preserve a feature of the Latin which the 1859 poem avoids, taking a safer and less interesting way. On the other hand, the second version establishes its own, plainer mode, less latinate in diction and somewhat less poetic in syntax. One can perhaps award points to the 1859 poem on the basis of "Thy knee bore long the leaves of ivy twined" *vs.* "Thy knee was bound with ivy" and "The baser breed . . . in puffy wooliness" *vs.* "The worse . . . their puffy fleeces glittering in the sun." This tendency of the later version toward plainness and away from the latinate word characterizes a stylistic ideal which is, I think, a just perceptible remove from the ideal of the first version. I find, for example, a consistent difference, but no obvious distinction of virtue, between "prepared for refutation" and "Half-ready now to swear it all away."

Despite our fondness for speaking of "the one, exact phrase" in poetry, and embarrassing or troublesome as the situation may be to the critic and scholar, neither translation of the *Idyllia* is merely a less good version of the other. The two must be studied, in some ways, as separate poems. Super dismisses all of the 1859 poems as "arid and prosaic," [13] but they often improve upon passages which seem very fine already in the 1847 version. I believe that this occurs slightly further on in "Pan and Pitys" from the passage just quoted. In lines 64–79, 1847, Pan defends himself; he never longed for Cynthia. Rather she, as one who loves sylvan beauty, wooed him:

> *"Not pleased too easily, unlovely things*
> *She shuns, by lovely (and none else) detain'd.*
> *Sweet, far above all birds, is philomel*
> *To her; above all scenes the Padan glades*
> *And their soft-whispering poplars; sweet to her*
> *The yellow light of box-tree in full bloom*
> *Nodding upon Cytoros. She delights*
> *To wander thro' the twinkling olive-grove,*
> *And when in clusters on Lycaean knolls*

13. *Ibid.,* p. 478.

> *Redden the berries of the mountain-ash;*
> *In glassy fountain, and grey temple-top,*
> *And smooth sea-wave, when Hesperus hath left*
> *The hall of Tethys, and when liquid sounds*
> *(Uncertain whence) are wafted to the shore . . .*
> *Never in Boreas."*

In the 1859 text, the same qualities which in the previous example produced an effect of relative thinness now produce an effect of relative crispness and vigor. Lines 59–71:

> *"not all*
> *Please her; she hates the rude, she cheers the gay,*
> *She shrouds her face when Boreas ventures near.*
> *Above all other birds the nightingale*
> *She loves; she loves the poplar of the Po*
> *Trembling and whispering; she descends among*
> *The boxtrees on Cytoros; night by night*
> *You find her at the olive: it is she*
> *Who makes the berries of the mountain-ash*
> *Bright at her touch: the glassy founts, the fanes*
> *Hoary with age, the sea when Hesper comes*
> *To Tethys, and when liquid voices rise*
> *Above the shore . . . but Boreas . . . no, not she."*

Certainly, the proper way to study these poems is not simply to cull one's preference between the two incarnations of each poem or passage; the procedure can become arrogant and tends to belittle Landor. I have used it to illustrate the nature of the two versions and to show that neither, strangely enough, can be dismissed. The situation is unique; whether or not Landor did forget the first translation, it seems certain that he did not consult it.

There is also the additional complication of the Latin originals. A worthwhile project as long as this book would be a detailed comparison of the three versions of each poem, revealing the apparent necessity of certain stylistic details to the poet's conception. Often, for instance, where the two English versions enjamb or end-stop on the same word, they reflect an apparently vital detail of the Latin. In this category is the full stop before "Wonderest" in each of the first pair of examples. And

the following lines in each version more or less duplicate the
line endings of:

> *Cur aperis oculos, similans nescire, paratus*
> *Cuncta regarduere et fontes celare Selini?*
> *"Pan et Pitys," lines 23–24*

In both English versions, the translation of "paratus" closes a
line; in both, the stop after "Selini" is imitated by a third-foot
caesura. Similarly, each rendering partly preserves, in a different way, the effect of:

> *Et mare, marmoreâ quando Hesperus exiit aulâ*
> *Tethyos, ac liquidae surgunt ad litora voces. . . .*

Even in the few dozen lines of these passages, there are several
such instances in which both translations choose the same line
or phrase for close imitation.

Of course, it is just possible that Landor forgot nothing and
simply decided that he would like to write the *Idyls* again. Cunningham's packet arrived, and the old man in his response
devised a way to have both his flattery and his revenge, by re-
fusing to correct Cunningham's misapprehension. Landor's
remark, in the letter which I have quoted, about "Whoever
may read or may not read them" is consistent with this interpretation of the facts. So are some other snippets of evidence: the
1847 *Hellenics* are subtitled "Enlarged and Completed," while
the 1859 volume, subtitled "New Edition, Enlarged," carefully
distinguishes by means of asterisks "works which are reprints
from the published works of the author; the others are either
new or have been rewritten" — thus putting the nine idylls into
an ambiguous category. There is no question, moreover, that
Landor had the existence of his 1847 volume of *Hellenics* very
firmly in mind, and the poems in question make up nearly two
thirds of that volume. In addition there is the negative evidence
that none of Landor's friends or admirers appears to have
expressed surprise at his double labor, accepting the 1859 poems
as conscious revisions. Landor's friend and biographer, John
Forster, who saw to the publishing of both volumes, writes:

Of those literary works under immediate notice the latest was the enlargement of his *Hellenics*; several new ones being added, and several of the old ones rewritten; but enough will have been said of it if I add that it had been especially his study, with advancing years, to give more and more of a severe and simple character to all his writing after the antique, and that this was exclusively the object, here, of the most part of his changes or additions.[14]

Forster seems very likely to be referring to the translated *Idyllia*; if he saw the *Gentleman's Magazine* for March, 1857, this passage would be consistent with knowledge that Landor's letter to Cunningham was a spoof. Landor's compliment to Cunningham there is perhaps explained by the attitude of a letter which Forster dates "1856":

We are living in a poetical world where atoms are flying up and down: where explosions are incessant: where bright buttons and unthreaded epaulettes, and laces of pantaloons and broken limbs in minute particles are scattered through the air . . . I venture to say this to you: to others I am a sad dissembler, and put on my sweetest smiles and prettiest behavior.[15]

It is possible that not only the praise of Cunningham's awful couplets, but also Landor's professed ignorance "that any man living could translate my Idylls," constituted a cynical, whimsical attitude toward the flying limbs and epaulettes among which his own work had been, by one man, forgotten in English and lauded in Latin.

Such a theory is a speculation without direct factual evidence, but that is nearly as true of the assumption that Landor forgot his own work. In support of that assumption there is the letter to Cunningham and there is the negative evidence that, as Super says, "nowhere does he show any sign of remembering that he has already published a translation of the ten Latin Idyls in the *Hellenics* of 1847."[16]

14. Forster, *Walter Savage Landor, A Biography* (London: Chapman and Hall, 1876), p. 489.

15. *Ibid.*, p. 501.

16. Super, *Walter Savage Landor*, p. 451. See, however, the testimony to Landor's lifelong bad memory in such matters given by his brother in

A strong tradition in the classical languages, that of translating and retranslating poetry, offered a precedent for Landor's project. And, in addition to a modified stylistic purpose, Landor might have had, as a reason for deliberate retranslation, a desire to work on longer pieces, to free his undiminished powers of composition from his flagging energy for invention. He continued to write at his best, and even perhaps to improve, through his old age; many of the best poems and anthology-pieces are extraordinarily late — including the poem "Memory," which, published when Landor was eighty-eight, treats the gradual oblivion of age with keen, burning self-awareness. Many of the most celebrated epigrams were composed after the poet was seventy, and his effortless command of the form endured well beyond seventy:

> *To my ninth decad I have tottered on,*
> *And no soft arm bends now my steps to steady;*
> *She, who once led me where she would, is gone,*
> *So when he calls me, Death shall find me ready.*

In fact, Landor's undiminished ability to write winning, pointed sentences in prose and verse weakens any argument which is based upon his senility. Super must demonstrate the weakness of old Landor's mind by quoting pungent letters like this one. (When Landor returned in considerable social disgrace to Italy, the addressee, of very old acquaintance, delivered some unknown slight):

> My lord, now I am recovering from an illness of several months' duration, aggravated no little by your lordship's rude reception of me at the Cascine, in presence of my family and numerous Florentines. I must remind you, in the gentlest terms, of the occurrence. It was the only personal indignity I ever received. We are both of us old men, my Lord, and verging on decrepitude and imbecility, else my note might be more energetic. Do not imagine I am unobservant of distinctions. You, by the grace

Forster, *Walter Savage Landor*, pp. 400–402. For example: "He continually denied that he had written what was to be found in his own books, or spoken what had been heard by twenty people" (p. 402).

of a Minister, are Marquis of Normanby; I by the Grace of God am Walter Savage Landor.[17]

What is mad in the letter characterized Landor from boyhood. The eccentricities of his old age were very much those he had practiced throughout life; tossing unsatisfactory meals (and an occasional cook) out the window; throwing insults in verse; advocating tyrannicide; deriding kings, priests, and archbishops; quarreling; fleeing (or, rather, abandoning) countries; and leaving his unpleasant wife. At eighty-four, he stabbed himself in a gesture of suicide, but he was vigorous enough to survive six years more; weeks after the stabbing he dramatically left home, stalking two and a half miles in the Italian sun. He continued at this time to rise early, to take long walks, and to read and write a great deal. If his follies increased with age, part of the cause was probably a shrewd but frustrated belief that he might die before the consequences arose. He was so self-indulgent all of his life, and retained so many extraordinary powers in old age, that one cannot assume his "senility" in a given matter.

If it could be proved that Landor intended the 1859 poems as complete revisions, and was merely spoofing Cunningham, then the proper procedure might be to use the 1859 text for all purposes. However, Super's thesis is the more likely, and I have suggested an alternative only because I think that the matter remains in doubt. My decision has been to use the 1847 poems as my principal text, because I prefer them. I quote in several places from the 1859 version to show that it embodies far more than a mere dilution, and to call attention to the discrepancies between the modern biographical conclusions and the modern textual procedures.

Whatever the truth of the muddle is, the relationship between the versions of Landor's *Idyllia* dramatizes one of the persistent themes of his career: the irresistible, doomed endeavor of inditing something which is already manifested but not yet grasped.

17. *Ibid.*, p. 466.

Moments or aggregates of experience, personal and historical, interested Landor as material known yet not perfected, to be reworked formally in the interest of permanence. The studying, translating, writing activities of the mind bore a peculiar intensity for him. This intensity is consistent with the old man's making anew the ideal mental poems about which swirled, in memory, the specific English and Latin lines of verse.

The Calm of Antiquity

A basic part of Landor's artistic credo is the attractive serenity acquired by fact, even the most passionate fact, as it moves into oblivious time. The credo dominates the *Hellenics*, where the aura of serenity, contrasted with violent, particular events, supports Landor's special stoicism. The consolation, the sureness, of this stoicism is to know what happened and to convert the knowledge into style, largely through an exquisite attention to physical details.

"Ye Who Have Toil'd" expresses a bitter commitment to this credo, as does another, very different poem, the "Apology for *Gebir*," which I discuss at the end of this book. That poem (which was written some sixty years after *Gebir*) combines Landor's concerns with the personal and the historical past. First, however, the background of the "Apology" must be completed by an examination of the ideal of calm which repeatedly appears as the end for which the poet or the hero toils.

Drastic, prolonged suffering, in two of Landor's dramatic poems, is the motive which drives his character, and the feeling of the work itself, toward a supernatural calm — although calm may not be the perfect word for so massive a release. The poems, containing the apotheosis-in-serenity of father and of son, are "The Prayer of Orestes" and "The Shades of Agamemnon and Iphigeneia." They constitute the final two scenes in a sequence of five treating the house of Atreus, a sequence which is opened by the lovely "Iphigeneia and Agamemnon." [18] That poem at once strikes a tone in which the impulse toward life-size, intimate character is balanced by a rich sense that this is the most venerable and high of tales:

> *Iphigeneia, when she heard her doom*
> *At Aulis, and when all beside the king*
> *Had gone away, took his right-hand, and said,*
> *"O father! I am young and very happy.*

The sequence as a whole sustains this tension between immediacy of emotion and a sense that the characters are august and remotely mythic. As a poetic form, it must be understood in the context of Romantic drama and, especially, Romantic tragedy.

Landor's idea of tragedy, like that of his contemporaries, was dominated by "the pathetic": tragedy, essentially, presents noble characters in the midst of great and powerfully affecting misfortune. Imitation is not so important as emotional persuasion. An emphasis upon moving the audience to the greatest, most painful degree of sympathy possible is reflected in Landor's remarks (and those of his contemporaries) on Shakespeare and on Greek tragedy. As plays like *Count Julian* plainly illustrate, such a concept of tragedy, although it may produce beautiful verse, fosters the neglect of more Aristotelian virtues.

The Romantic tragedian, concentrating on the audience's delight in being swept away, proportionately fails to exploit the delight which comes from an awareness that one is witnessing an imitation. Character is more important than plot — or, if that is too banal a way of saying it, character as dominant, lyric personality is more important than character as the driving force of a whole form. Although one can find nearly any theo-

18. I am considering the poems as published in the 1847 *Hellenics*, with this poem (the only one not a dialogue) not separated from the other four as it later was. Although the poems stand separately and were meant to do so, I think that their publication as a sequence — from which "Iphigeneia" may have been broken through an oversight — justifies so considering them. ("Iphigeneia and Agamemnon," also called "Iphigeneia"; "The Death of Clytaemnestra"; "The Madness of Orestes"; "The Prayer of Orestes"; and "The Shades of Agamemnon and Iphigeneia.")

retical position on the subject in Hazlitt, Coleridge, or De Quincey, the age's bias is entirely apparent in the practice of its dramatists.[19] And Landor shared that bias; if his plays are among the finest tragedies of their period (as I suppose they must be), they still remain, like Shelley's *The Cenci*, Keats' *Otho the Great*, and Byron's *Sardanapalus*, formally meaning-less. That is, the plot has no meaning as an arrangement of inci-dents: it is a means of attempting one great, climactic scene after another.

In the dramatic scene or *agon*, however, Landor discovered a form better suited to an art which in full-length drama empha-sized the great scene almost to the exclusion of plot, and plot's context of causality. Dealing with the family whose story is the most familiar of tragic materials, he could in a compact work develop his theme of time's dual effects — corrosive and monu-mental. These lyric-dramatic poems reflect the tendencies of Romantic tragedy in the stormy intensity which precedes their final calm. The madness of Landor's Orestes is dire, violent, and meant to overwhelm. Like most of the emotions in the sequence, it is meant in part to represent pure passion — turbulent human passion itself; it is the restless curse of feeling, an inspiration from which the individual would be free:

> Orestes. *O king Apollo! god Apollo! god*
> *Powerful to smite and powerful to preserve!*
> *If there is blood upon me, as there seems,*
> *Purify that black stain (thou only canst)*
> *With every rill that bubbles from these caves*
> *Audibly; and come willing to the work.*
> *No; 'tis not they; 'tis blood; 'tis blood again*
> *That bubbles in my ear, that shakes the shades*
> *Of thy dark groves, and lets in hateful gleams,*
> *Bringing me . . . what dread sight! what sounds abhorr'd!*
> *What screams! They are my mother's: 'tis her eye*
> *That through the snakes of those three furies glares,*
> *And makes them hold their peace that she may speak.*
> *Has thy voice bidden them all forth? There slink*

19. See also, for example, the bias toward moving men "to true sympathy" in Shelley's preface to *The Cenci*.

Some that would hide away, but must turn back,
And others like blue lightnings bound along
From rock to rock; and many hiss at me
As they draw nearer. Earth, fire, water, all
Abominate the deed the Gods commanded!
Alas! I came to pray, not to complain;
And lo! my speech is impious as my deed.
                    "The Prayer of Orestes," lines 1–21

    Orestes. . . . *Hiss me not back*
Ye snake-hair'd maids! I will look on; I will
Hear the words gurgle thro' that cursed stream,
And catch that hand . . . that hand . . . which slew my father!
. . . .

                    I am not yours
Fell Goddesses! A just and generous Power,
A bright-hair'd God, directed me.
                    And thus
Abased is he whom such a God inspired!
        "The Madness of Orestes," lines 16–19, 35–39

Mingled passion and duty comprise the constantly enormous burden of the Romantic hero. He is, like the Romantic poet, inspired — possessed — by a superhuman charge of feeling. With such a scheme of the tragic emotion, recognition is perpetual, and the audience must always believe that the crescendo is at its peak. There is no room for the gradual discovery of Lear or Oedipus. The scene is the thing, and the speech.

This literary explanation of the inadequacies of Romantic tragedy is perhaps tautological, but it does suggest why the emotion packed verse-scene was a natural and successful venture for Landor. A less obvious, philosophical explanation offered in George Steiner's well-known book, *The Death of Tragedy*, harmonizes with the strictly literary theory, and Steiner's view of Romantic tragedy also helps to clarify Landor's ideal of calm.

Steiner lists Landor along with Blake, Wordsworth, Scott, Coleridge, Southey, Hunt, Shelley, Keats, and Beddoes; all wrote or began tragedies, often with the very highest hopes. The purpose of Steiner's list is

to suggest the magnitude of implied aspiration and effort. Here
we find some of the masters of the language producing tragedies
which are, with few signal exceptions, dismally bad.[20]

A principal explanation for such recurrent failure is, he continues, Rousseauistic optimism. Man in the Romantic era "was,
in the vocabulary of romanticism, perfectible." And the moral
correlative of this belief was a transformation in the idea of
guilt; guilt is no longer a final state of knowledge, but a stage
toward spiritual triumph. "Crime leads not to punishment but
to redemption." Steiner cites the excellent examples of *The
Ancient Mariner, Les Miserables,* and the crucial difference of
Goethe's *Faust* from that of Marlowe. He then traces this evasion of the tragic logic in the plays of several English Romantics.

Now, Landor was as much as any of his generation a partici-
pant in the new "dawn" (as Wordsworth, quoted by Steiner,
called it) of optimistic liberalism. He was at least as committed
to a scheme of tragedy in which *having emotion* — the condition
of passion, rather than an ideal of kingship or duty — is the
hero's distinguishing burden. Finally, like his fellow dramatists,
Landor did not command a religious or fatalistic sense of universal order. This absence of a convincing Necessity, in works so
profoundly influenced by Shakespeare, results in the curious
slackness of Romantic tragedies: the violent passions presented
are well enough justified internally, by the causal relationships
of the story, but a quality of aimlessness emerges from the lack of
any stringent external ordering.

But he differed in this: Landor was less willing than the
author of *The Ancient Mariner,* or that of *The Borderers,* to
create spiritual values where he did not find them. His dramas
do sometimes show the Romantic interest in an escape from
tragedy by way of remorse and redemption, but the tendency
is, as in *Fra Rupert,* abortive. The ideal of political renascence

20. George Steiner, *The Death of Tragedy* (London: Faber and Faber,
1961), pp. 122–25. The list is impressive enough, but a few paragraphs later
we find still more names of illustrious failures; Browning, Dickens, Tennyson, Swinburne, George Meredith, Stendahl, Balzac, Flaubert, Zola, Dos-
toevsky, Henry James.

in the other plays is finally inadequate as the "compensating heaven" which (if we accept the theory for this discussion) is a requisite of Romantic tragedy.[21] In the Atreus scenes, the compensating heaven which serves in the place of pre-Romantic ideals of order is calm: an affirmation that time will bring release from the "impious," raging passion which is Orestes' burden and Agamemnon's.

Simply to call this theme stoic is insufficient because the elements of desperation and regret are so strong, and because the treatment is so intense — often excessively so. Yet the poems persuade; the short, near-lyric form suits the theme of eventual peace as the unravelling of a full drama could not. And despite their faults they help define the full emotional meaning of Landor's characteristic detachment — or rather, his hunger for detachment and peace.

Orestes' speech in "The Prayer of Orestes" (quoted above) is answered by a chorus in ode stanzas spoken by a priestess of Apollo. Like the comforting and tormenting Eumenides, Apollo plays the double role of inspiring the hero's passion and releasing him from it. Orestes' anguish is balanced by the cool movement of this hymn; the closing promise that mythic fame will bring him rest is balanced by mention of the mocking boys, which maintains some element of Orestes as more human, more vulnerable than the sheer name which he will become. This indignity is worse than Aegisthus', although not as awful. It is the particular and the present with which one suffers most. The chant consists of a long sentence which stretches its graceful skein between the two shorter periods both of which contain a promise of rest:

21. Steiner believes that "beyond the tragic, there lies no 'happy ending' in some other dimension of place or time," and quotes I. A. Richards, who says that the mind

> does not shy away from anything, it does not protect itself with any illusion, it stands uncomforted, alone and self reliant. . . . The least touch of any theology which has a compensating Heaven to offer the tragic hero is fatal.

Orestes: *Earth, fire, water, all*
Abominate the deed the Gods commanded!
Alas! I came to pray, not to complain;
And lo! my speech is impious as my deed!

                     Priestess of Apollo
Take refuge here amid our Delphian shades,
        O troubled breast!
Here the most pious of Mycenai's maids
        Shall watch thy rest
And wave the cooling laurel o'er thy brow,
        Nor insect swarm
Shall ever break thy slumbers, nor shalt thou
        Start at the alarm
Of boys infesting (as they do) the street
        With mocking songs,
Stopping and importuning all they meet,
        And heaping wrongs
Upon thy diadem'd and sacred head,
        Worse than when base
Aegisthus (shudder not!) his toils outspread
        Around thy race.
Altho' even in this fane the fitful blast
        Thou may'st hear roar,
Thy name among our highest rocks shall last
        For evermore.

Despite such inessentials as ("shudder not!") the exclamation marks, the writing has an irresistible quality of song. It also represents an attempt to redefine the tragic solace in the terms of Landor's own credo: "Even in this fane . . ." the wind of suffering is heard. The ideal is not of escape or rest, exactly, but of calm. Orestes' agony persists, even though Orestes dies. And in a way, Suffering-Orestes lives. Time heals by destroying, but time also preserves, for one's passions — if one happens to be a hero — attain an immutable quality.

I think that the intended effect — the significance for non-heroic reader and writer — is a recognition that there is some measure of compensating justice in time's dual working. The feeling is much softer, and less satisfying, than catharsis; the solace is, as in "Death of Day," meager, bitter. Calm is not a vacuity, but has kinds. The Landorian calm is not a purgation of suffering but a containment of it within a sense that suffering passes — and, being over, does not change; myths constitute the most powerful emblem of this limited solace. If Orestes' trials are of sufficiently heroic stature, and if subsequent minds toil with sufficient skill to conceive the facts properly, then Orestes moves into the peace of myth as well as that of death. That process is reflected on the personal level by the stoic comfort which verse of the correct tone gives to loss or distress.

The importance of poetry, of myth, and of true tonal knowledge in this attitude suggests comparison of Landor with the Aesthetes of later generations. His method is very far from mere sentimentalization of the past; if art tends to become a religion, it is worshipped as clear vision, not as beautiful sensation. Nevertheless, the affinity is there: Swinburne uses the word "relief" to describe his long-standing love of a chorus (very similar in function to the priestess' song above) in the next and final poem of the Atreus sequence:

> his poems had first given me inexplicable pleasure and a sort of blind relief when I was a small fellow of twelve. My first recollection of them is *The Song of the Hours* in the Iphigeneia [i.e., "The Shades of Agamemnon and Iphigeneia"].[22]

22. Quoted by Super, *Walter Savage Landor*, p. 613. Swinburne continues, revealing his reaction against the quasi-religious, Unitarian kind of poetry which Landor, too, so contemned:

> Apart from this executive perfection, all those Greek poems of his always fitted on to my own way of feeling and thought infinitely more than even Tennyson's modern versions do now. I am more than ever sure that the *Hamadryad* is a purer and better piece of work, from the highest point of view that art can take, than such magnificent hashes and stews of old and new with a sharp sauce of personality as *Oenone* and *Ulysses*. Not that I am disloyal to Tennyson, into whose church we were all in my time born and baptized as far back as we can remember at all. But he is not a Greek nor a heathen, and I imagine does not want to be. I greatly fear he believes it possible to be something better; an absurdity which should be left to the Brownings and other blatant creatures begotten on the slime of the modern chaos.

He thought this "divine" poem to be "the crown of all the *Hellenics*" (Malcolm Elwin, *Landor, A Replevin* [London: Macdonald, 1958], p. 364).

These ideas, just emergent in "The Prayer of Orestes," are much more apparent in "The Shades of Agamemnon and Iphigeneia." The movement-into-stillness of Orestes is simply his death, on the basic level; his answer to the priestess begins:

> *A calm comes over me: life brings it not*
> *With any of its tides: my end is near.*
> *O Priestess of the purifying God, . . .*

But in the final poem of the sequence Landor devises a much more intricate fable.

The poem's protagonist is Agamemnon, who in the initial poem, "Iphigeneia and Agamemnon" (earlier titled "Iphigeneia") was a silent, terrifying foil for Iphigeneia's monologue. His special agony in this poem arises from Landor's rather strange fictional invention. His rejuvenation of a very ancient kind of dialogue — the discourse of famous shades — is sanctioned by the following speech of Aeschylus' Clytaemnestra:

> *There will be no tears in this house for him.*
> *It must be Iphigeneia*
> *his child, who else,*
> *shall greet her father by the whirling stream*
> *and the ferry of tears*
> *to close him in her arms and kiss him.*[23]

It is a very ironic speech, since this is in Clytaemnestra's eyes the daughter whom Agamemnon "dealt with even as he has suffered."[24]

In Landor's poem, Iphigeneia greets her father with the greatest affection, but he is tormented by the situation: Iphigeneia knows nothing of what has happened and almost at once asks about her dear mother. Agamemnon's anguish is compounded by his knowledge that Iphigeneia must now be told of his murder:

> Agamemnon. *O Earth! I suffered less upon thy shores!*
> *(Aside.) The bath that bubbled with my blood, the blows*

23. Aeschylus, *Agamemnon*, trans. Richmond Lattimore, in *Greek Tragedies*, ed. David Grene and Richmond Lattimore, 3 vols. (Chicago: University of Chicago Press, 1960), vol. 1, p. 55, II, 1553–59.
24. *Ibid.*, 2:1526–27.

> *That spilt it (O worse torture!) must she know?*
> *Ah! the first woman coming from Mycneai*
> *Will pine to pour this poison in her ear,*
> *Taunting sad Charon for his slow advance.*

They converse, each understanding little of what the other says. The asides are many, and although Iphigeneia does not understand the exact circumstances and events of the tragedy, her father betrays an even greater ignorance of its final spirit. Iphigeneia knows that shades do not suffer mortal emotions as mortals do; they know passions, but do not feel them. As Aspasia says in introducing the poem, "Love is not a stranger in Elysium, but suffering is."[25]

The question of how much passion is felt among the shades dominates the poem from their first greeting. "We are not shades / Surely!" says Iphigeneia as he grasps her hand, "for yours throbs yet!" She then mentions Clytaemnestra, and also says that it was "ill done" in herself to shrink with fear when killed by the priest. Agamemnon responds with the dominant theme:

> Agamemnon. *Ye Gods who govern here! do human pangs*
> *Reach the pure soul thus far below? do tears*
> *Spring in these meadows?*
> Iphigeneia.   *No, sweet father, no . . .*
> *I could have answered that; why ask the Gods?*

He is skeptical because of what he knows, replying that

> *the Earth*
> *Has gendered crimes unheard-of heretofore,*
> *And Nature may have changed in her last depths,*
> *Together with the Gods and all their laws.*

And the repeated movement of the poem, up to the chorus, is a tugging between her fervid promises of peace and his savage, disbelieving pain.

Although the subject is tranquility, the conception, the fiery style, and the mode of the writing all illustrate how emptily one might speak of "Landorian reserve." Landor, as here, al-

25. Landor, *Works*, 10:227.

ways pushes each feeling to its extreme, going over the edge in more than one poem; he expresses even the ideal of aloofness in the most extravagant, absolute terms ("I strove with *none* . . .").

But the strange plan of this lyric conversation is not merely a platform for excited rhetoric. Neither, although it nearly staggers under its freight of situational ironies, is the odd setting deliberately bizarre, for the sake of merely clever involution. And Landor makes no Wordsworth-like speculations about the afterlife, a subject upon which he had no opinion.

Rather, the eschatology is a symbolic medium for certain ethical concerns: what, emotionally, does it mean to long for tranquillity? If oblivion of some sort is the only escape from passion, then the only peace is in death, or inanition. To put it differently, Landor is trying to imagine a sustaining forcefulness, useful to life, in the fact that time ends many human concerns; he is trying to imagine a tenable tone for the statement, "Time heals passions." To be acceptable, such an idea or imagined tone must allow that in some sense the passion survives. Aspasia (introducing the work as her own) says:

> Nothing, I confess, would be more ill-placed than a *Drama* or *Dialogue* in the world below; at least, if the shades entered into captious disquisitions or frivolous pleasantries. But we believe that our affections outlive us. . . . Humours, the idioms of life, are lost in the transition, or are generalized in the concourse and convergency of innumerable races: passions, the universal speech, are thoroughly intelligible.[26]

Characteristically, the problem finds expression in a metaphor of style and language, and here we cannot untangle vehicle and tenor, because for Landor serious ethical questions were problems of tone and definition and every stylistic problem was an ethical trial of the man. To find the right way to say a thing is to feel the right way about it.

Therefore, to imagine shades who can recall their lives, yet

26. *Ibid.*

remain at peace, would be to reconcile and evaluate one's fear that time removes human feeling, and one's fear that time will not. The poem is governed by a tension, an uncertainty whether Agamemnon will be persuaded, and whether Iphigeneia will find herself moved. How, after all, can he break his awful news, within the scheme which Landor has created? She is, it is underlined, far from unfeeling, and the language of the blank verse is the opposite of cool. As in his shorter lyrics, the Horatian calm appears as a hunger rather than a tone, so in this poem the reward of peace appears to be in abeyance. When Agamemnon speaks of unheard-of crimes, saying that "Nature may have changed in her last depths,/Together with the Gods and all their laws," she responds:

> *Father! we must not let you here condemn;*
> *Not, were the day less joyful: recollect*
> *We have no wicked here; no king to judge.*
> *Poseidon, we have heard, with bitter rage*
> *Lashes his foaming steeds against the skies,*
> *And, laughing with loud yell at winged fire*
> *Innoxious to his fields and palaces,*
> *Affrights the eagle from the sceptred hand;*
> *While Pluto, gentlest brother of the three*
> *And happiest in obedience, views sedate*
> *His tranquil realm, nor envies theirs above.*
> *No change have we, not even day for night*
> *Nor spring for summer.*
>   *All things are serene,*
> *Serene too be your spirit! None on earth*
> *Ever was half so kindly in his house. . . .*

Pluto, toward whose realm all things tend, presents peace, but it is a peace which Iphigeneia defines stirringly by means of its opposite.

Conceptually, the important part of her speech is, "No change have we," for that statement points the way out of Landor's seemingly insoluble situation. Our suspense, at last, will be deflected, not met. But first, Agamemnon's changed understanding of the situation begins at about this point, with comprehension that Iphigeneia's love for him truly is unchanged, contradicting Clytaemnestra's terrible prediction. He apostrophizes her defiantly, reaching the crucial idea of permanence at his speech's close.

> *Fell woman! ever false! false was thy last*
> *Denunciation, as thy bridal vow;*
> *And yet even that found faith with me! The dirk*
> *Which sever'd flesh from flesh, where this hand rests,*
> *Severs not, as thou boastedst in your scoffs,*
> *Iphigeneia's love from Agamemnon:*
> *The daughter's not her heart's whole fount hath quencht,*
> *'Tis worthy of the Gods, and lives for ever.*

The great number of tropes in this speech reveal the impending climax. These almost Elizabethan rhetorical figures ("And yet even that found faith," the play on "severs," "her heart's whole fount") are managed with taste and strength. They achieve a rigor of attention which usually, in the *Hellenics*, arises from realistic physical detail — in this poem, such details are suppressed, for excellent reasons.

Agamemnon is still torn by Iphigeneia's innocence and seeming vulnerability. Midway in her next speech, she reminds him, and herself, that

> *We are shades!*
> *Groan not thus deeply; blight not thus the season*
> *Of full-orb'd gladness! Shades we are indeed,*
> *But mingled, let us feel it, with the blest.*

And Agamemnon, realizing now what "never changing" means, responds in a speech in which the blank verse crackles, charged in the rhythm of its first line almost to the breaking point; each word bears great stress until the release on "Iphigeneia." To hear the pentameter throb through this line, it helps to have the preceding one, Iphigeneia's:

> *Save one, who loves me most, and most would chide me.*
>   Agamemnon. *We want not, O Iphigeneia, we*
> *Want not embrace, nor kiss that cools the heart*
> *With purity, nor words that more and more*
> *Teach what we know from those we know, and sink*
> *Often most deeply where they fall most light.*

> *Time was when for the faintest breath of thine*
> *Kingdom and life were little.*
>   Iphigeneia.   *Value them*
> *As little now.*

The speech prepares us for the evasion of our suspense which is about to come; it is also very beautifully and subtly written. The "we" stressed by a hovering accent the first time, and by a superb runover the second time, emphasizes the special state which they share, as Agamemnon is now coming to understand. The word "want," meaning primarily "lack," retains a touch of its meaning as "desire," and their freedom in desiring nothing, yet having what they desire, is so emphasized. He need desire nothing for her — not, any longer, breath itself.

These are characters on a very figurative level, characters who in a way feel themselves becoming abstractions. They are not in time; Iphigeneia can learn, will learn, nothing. They cannot dread. He answers her speech above with the wish, "Were life and kingdom all!" And she reminds him that while Electra and Orestes may mourn and suffer,

> *They will be happy too.*
>   *Cheer! king of men!*
> *Cheer! there are voices, songs. Cheer! arms advance.*
>   Agamemnon. *Come to me, soul of peace! These, these alone,*
> *These are not false embraces.*
>   Iphigeneia.   *Both are happy!*
>   Agamemnon. *Freshness breathes round me from some breeze above.*
> *What are ye, winged ones! with golden urns?*

And so the first half of the poem ends with an odd retreat, a lyric relaxation rather than a dramatic fulfillment of tension. These shades are not people, but symbols, and the exact significance of what has happened is next made clear. Agamemnon's question is answered by the chorus which Swinburne associated with his feeling "a sort of blind relief."

> *The Hours . . To each an urn we bring.*
> *Earth's purest gold*
> *Alone can hold*
> *The lymph of the Lethean spring.*

We, son of Atreus! we divide
The dulcet from the bitter tide
      That runs across the paths of men.
No more our pinions shalt thou see.
Take comfort! We have done with thee,
And must away to earth again.

The familiar theme: the boundless peace of every past event is that every event is touched by the hours only once. What is over does not change.

In "Memory," the waters of forgetfulness tear up flowers as well as weeds, and the same idea therefore appears as a very black one because its application is personal, its context that of affection. Here, the application is heroic, and the context is torment, so the effect is optimistic, or at least redemptive: what is noble and heroic is not forgotten, although the particulars of human suffering are. For heroes, and heroic passions, weeds and flowers are *not* alike tugged into Lethe's current.

Iphigeneia, symbol of innocence, of sacrificed joy, and now of unchanging calm, gives the old hero that peace which became hers at the end of the first poem, where she progressed from "O father! I am young and very happy" to her final resignation: "O father! grieve no more: the ships can sail." What thou lovest well remains, in the sense that what is heroic is by definition that which remains most surely engraved in personal or cultural memory. Just as "the fairest form" avoided the death of day because she fell to a sterner death, Iphigeneia died untouched by the future shame; but more important, she epitomizes death-with-purpose, and the progress of passion to impersonal clarity.

Landor in these poems, then, is redefining ancient ideals of duty, heroic stature, and Elysian calm, all in the context of Romantic consolation. If the Romantic hero's burden of emotion attains absolute, heroic purity, full circle is completed, and he trades human misery and happiness for the dignity of marble. "The pathetic" is balanced by the heroic, and these final poems balance such earlier moments as Iphigeneia's plea:

I thought to have laid down my hair before
Benignant Artemis, and not have dimm'd
Her polisht altar with my virgin blood.
   "Iphigeneia and Agamemnon," lines 26–28

It is familiar for a Romantic poet, in the absence of a positive relief from suffering, to worship suffering itself, to put a value on emotion for its own sake. What is unique here is the combination of this tendency with an ideal of detachment. Neither is Landor's poem a mere Romantic idealization of antiquity, although it does include an element resembling such sentimentalization. To all of this, the idea of heroic stature is vitally important, which explains why the subsequent choruses are nearly as long as the poem proper, the dialogue itself. These choruses begin as the hours reascend, affirming as they do the importance of Iphigeneia: the one who died, who made possible the Argive glory, and who brooded over the subsequent suffering, already in the mythic past:

> *Where thou art, thou*
> *Of braided brow,*
> *Thou cull'd too soon from Argive bow'rs*
> *Where thy sweet voice is heard among*
> *The shades that thrill with choral song,*
> *None can regret the parted hours.*

The rest of the chorus is that of Argive warriors, who begin by hailing Iphigeneia, "the spirit that breathes/ Triumph and joy" into their song: "Iphigeneia! 'tis to thee/Glory we owe and victory." The verse of these choruses is suitably vigorous:

> *We too, thou seest, are now*
> *Among the happy, though the aged brow*
> *From sorrow for us we could not protect,*
>   *Nor, on the polisht granite of the well*
>   *Folding our arms, of spoils and perils tell,*
> *Nor lift the vase on the lov'd head erect.*

> *Semichorus*
> *What whirling wheels are those behind?*
> *What plumes come flaring through the wind,*
>   *Nearer and nearer? From his car*

He who defied the heaven-born powers of war
Pelides springs: Dust, dust are we
To him, O king, who bends the knee,
Proud only to be first in reverent praise of thee.

But as the Argive force appears, the final exalted evocation is not of Achilles, but of another hero: one whose career and end epitomizes grand, temporal folly. The course taken by his "insatiate soul" represents that which governs the sequence as a whole:

Chorus

Hark! from afar more war-steeds neigh,
Thousands o'er thousands rush this way.
Ajax is yonder! ay, behold
The radiant arms of Lycian gold!
Arms from admiring valor won,
Tydeus! and worthy of thy son.
'Tis Ajax wears them now; for he
Rules over Adria's stormy sea.

He threw them to the friend who lost
(By the dim judgment of the host)
Those wet tears which Thetis gave
The youth most beauteous of the brave.
In vain! the insatiate soul would go
For comfort to his peers below.
Clash! ere we leave them all the plain,
Clash! Io Paean! once again!

And so the poem ends. The choruses in "The Prayer of Orestes" and "The Shades of Agamemnon and Iphigeneia" embody or conduct a change of state. This change from temporal suffering to timeless tranquillity is a nineteenth-century reflection of the tragic movement of the *Oresteia* itself, from Furies to Eumenides. The Greek original's movement from communal chaos toward justice is reflected, in Landor's work, by a movement from emotional distraction toward clarity; catharsis, the audience's sympathetic feeling of integrity with the cosmos, is reflected by relief, the paler and more restricted feeling of integrity with one's own emotions.

To put it more plainly, Landor's Orestes seeks to set right his own condition, not a whole state of things. We are told that he is a hero, as is necessary, but the scenes in which we see him portray a search for personal relief. This is what comes after tragedy, or, perhaps, is subordinate to it.

The way in which the original *Oresteia* is reflected, then, adds a further interest to these poems; I believe that Landor was aware of that element in them.[27] Such an awareness is consistent with his practice as I have attempted to describe it. The procedure's humility explains the relative success of what might seem a hopelessly audacious endeavor.

Landor's Atreus sequence is composed of very strange, frequently very beautiful poems. They are also imperfect. The difficult questions raised are to a great extent begged; despite Swinburne's "blind relief," the poems do not solve the problem stated by "Memory," as they sometimes apparently promise to do. Instead they state the problem in a way that is very satisfying tonally, in the form of an agonized revery. As in "Tintern Abbey," the despair is more moving than the affirmation — is implicit in the affirmation. Swinburne's phrase is in this sense exactly right: we find tonal relief rather than a "visible" solution.

The relief rests upon an ancient ideal and, very characteristically, upon an ancient and very celebrated plot. These acquire certain special qualities by being combined with such Romantic ideas as the sanctity of emotion itself. An awareness of Landor's concerns helps to clarfy the poem's form: although the chorus of Argives, for example, is probably too long, it is very lovely, and suited to a very definite purpose. Conversely, a receptive approach to such odd-seeming formal elements allows one to see the poem's seriousness, obviating the critic's judgment that in the *Hellenics* "Landor no longer has much to say except that young love is sweet."[28]

27. See Aspasia's self-deprecation, her peculiar, rather contradictory remarks about "the pathetic," and the tears that she wept while writing the poem.

28. Douglas Bush, *Mythology and the Romantic Tradition in English Poetry* (Cambridge, Mass.: Harvard University Press, 1937), p. 239.

Antiquity and Contemporary Politics

The same critic quotes (from another context) and applies to
Landor the statement "I don't see any internal centre from
which springs anything which he does."²⁹ If I have labored
certain themes in this book, it has been to show that Landor's
"internal centre" is so evident as to be invisible. He respected
the past, and we tend to assume that we know what *that* means:
Classicism, statuary, and so forth. I think that the Atreus poems
fill out a definition of several related themes — calm, the heroic
past, the contrasted pain of temporal existence. These themes
have an urgent solemnity which was Landor's familiarly, by
virtue of the unique thoroughness and depth of his culture.
Without his power to make poetry in English, Latin, and Greek,
and without his scholarship in other matters, we may nevertheless understand the seriousness of his themes, because his poems
persuade. And so the Elysium of his Iphigeneia sheds light on
many other poems.

This is true, I think, not only of such familiar, minor examples as "Ternissa, You Are Fled," in which the peace of the
dead, contrasted with the longing of the living, is expressed in
old mythology, and in the slow tune of the long, final line:

> *And your cool palm smoothes down stern Pluto's cheek,*

or, in another familiar poem, where something like the reverse
occurs, and the closing lines gain timbre from a knowledge of
Landor's "internal centre." The longing is no retreat:

> *never waste their hours*
> *(Ardent for action) among meadow flowers.*
> *Greece with calm eyes I see.*
> *Her pure white marbles have not blinded me,*
> *But breathe on me the love*
> *Of earthly things as bright as things above:*
> *There is (where is there not?)*
> *In her fair regions many a desert spot;*
> *Neither is Dirce clear,*
> *Nor is Ilissus full throughout the year.*

29. *Ibid.,* p. 233. George Meredith on Swinburne.

In such poems we take a pleasure, familiar in Landor's work, in seeing how the frightened personal perception of time combines with aloof historical perception of time, producing a graceful, although fragile, tone of voice.

But the theme of the past, even considered in its most narrow and most impersonal sense as immersion in antiquity, functions in less obvious ways as well. In two poems of very similar structure, a brief, extremely immediate evocation of an ancient moment appears approximately midway. In both cases the vivid mythical scene throws a more or less "political" subject into long perspective.

In a way, the political statement thus acquires a background of Augustan wisdom; all things change, and the present which seems so vivid is but one moment in eternity. Yet the atmosphere of the mythical scene is in neither poem coolly Augustan; the calm of the centuries is entirely implicit, assumed, and the contemporary statement gathers most of its emotional source through association with the myth. This technique, in its economy and assurance, makes much twentieth-century "use of myth" — all of the Oedipuses and Medeas clothed in modern dress or existential philosophy — seem gauche.

More similar is the procedure of certain moments in *The Waste Land*, which Landor's technique as I have described it may call to mind. However, the resemblance is superficial; Landor's tone is not allusive, elegiac, or hesitant; the past is real, violently real, and more real in fact than the shadowy, slavelike present:

> here Aegeus cried,
> "Oh Sun! careering over Sipylus,
> If desolation (worse than ever there
> Befell the mother, and those heads her own
> Would shelter, when the deadly darts flew round)
> Impend not o'er my house, in gloom so long,
> Let one swift cloud illumined by the chariot
> Sweep off the darkness from that doubtful sail!"
>
> Deeper and deeper came the darkness down;
> The sail itself was heard; his eyes grew dim:

> *His knees tottered beneath him, but availed*
> *To bear him till he plunged into the deep.*
>
> *Sound, fifes! there is a youthfulness of sound*
> *In your shrill voices: sound again, ye lips*
> *That Mars delights in. I will look no more*
> *Into the time behind for idle goads*
> *To stimulate faint fancies: hope itself*
> *Is bounded by the starry zone of glory.*
> *On one bright point we gaze, one wish we breathe:*
>
> *Athens! be ever as thou art this hour,*
> *Happy and strong, a Pericles thy guide.*
> *"Sophocles to Poseidon," lines 8–27* [30]

Such acute details as the sound of the sail, and the hope that the sail is a white one shadowed by a cloud, are hallmarks of Landor's peculiar realism. Here they are wedded closely to the poem's theme: change, looked for in the wind, the sun, the color of the sail flown by a careless son. Greece, like the Aegean, has changed and will change many times:

> *The colours of the waves are not the same*
> *Day after day, Poseidon! nor the same*
> *The fortunes of the land wherefrom arose*
> *Under thy trident the brave friend of man.*
> *lines 1–4*

And so Sophocles' change from old images of despair to new joyfulness is both ironic and affirmed: ironic because bad days will return to Periclean Greece and affirmed because better ones will return to modern Greece. And paradoxically, the heroic stature of the old grief adds a buoyant, full resonance to the optimism. An emphasis on the present prayer, with mere reference to the Aegean as heroic setting, would have been feeble, a stale literary posture. But the familiarity of that posture enables Landor to work in such quick, large strokes. His full-blooded gloss on the word "Aegean" puts present ills in their place at the same time as it renders them more poignant.

30. Both poems were attached to conversations; both were published independently in the *Hellenics*. "Sophocles to Poseidon" goes with "Pericles and Sophocles," "To Corinth" with "Maurocordato and Colocotroni."

The companion-poem "To Corinth" is spoken in Landor's own voice and concludes with a much more explicit and firmly colored vision of nineteenth-century politics. The poem opens, however, with a very similar invocation of the particular place which binds the present to the past. Although the past itself is not calm or dim, the intervening years embodied in the locale are the soul of calm. The air of ceremony in this opening is an important aspect of the poem's effect; it is contrasted with the fierce turbulence of the conclusion. This tone stands in relation to the later one as does the cliff to the waves and "seen generations" below. By the end, we will join them, but we begin with a hymn:

> *Queen of the double seas, beloved of him*
> *Who shakes the world's foundations, thou hast seen*
> *Glory in all her beauty, all her forms;*
> *Seen her walk back with Theseus when he left*
> *The bones of Sciron bleaching in the wind,*
> *Above the ocean's roar and cormorant's flight,*
> *So high that vastest billows from above*
> *Show but like herbage waving in the mead;*
> *Seen generations throng thy Isthmian games,*
> *And pass away; the beautiful, the brave,*
> *And them who sang their praises. But, O Queen,*
> *Audible still, and far beyond thy cliffs . . . .*
>
> *lines 1–12*

After the scene of Jason and Medea there is a transition to the conclusion, which seems a return from horror back to ceremony, but the hymn ends with startling violence; we go from Jason and the murdered children to statuary, and from there to nineteenth-century Europe — yet the tonal decorum is sustained.

> *He* [Jason] *was more changed than they were, doomed to show*
> *Thee and the stranger, how defac'd and scarr'd*
> *Grief hunts us down the precipe of years,*
> *And whom the faithless prey upon the last.*
> *   To give the inertest masses of our earth*
> *Her loveliest forms, was thine; to fix the Gods*
> *Within thy walls, and hang their tripods round*
> *With fruits and foliage knowing not decay.*

A nobler work remains: thy citadel
Invites all Greece: o'er lands and floods remote
Many are the hearts that still beat high for thee:
Confide then in thy strength, and unappall'd
Look down upon the plain, while yokemate kings
Run bellowing where their herdsmen goad them on.
Instinct is sharp in them and terror true,
They smell the floor whereon their necks must lie.
lines 32–46

The violence is justified by the madness of European politics at the time and by the counterbalancing violence of the older Corinth. Because the latter is contained within the unchanging aura of the locale, so too is the former. The scene is very thoroughly realized, staying from excess the image of rulers as crazed oxen. The antiquity of "fruits and foliage knowing not decay" also supplies a more awful image of crime and dishonor breeding themselves:

"Medea! Is that blood? again! it drops
From my imploring hand upon my feet!
I will invoke the Eumenides no more,
I will forgive thee, bless thee, bend to thee
In all thy wishes, but do thou, Medea,
Tell me, one lives."
"And shall I too deceive?"
Cries from the fiery car an angry voice;
And swifter than two falling stars descend
Two breathless bodies; warm, soft, motionless
As flowers in stillest noon before the sun,
They lie three paces from him. . . .
lines 18–28

The moment of infanticide, remote and stylized by time as we know it to be, is nonetheless real and awful. Only the cliff, Corinth, intervening time itself, suggests the stillness of statuary, a height which recalls the upper air "where curlews soar" in "Ye Who Have Toil'd." The skepticism of that poem fosters the technique of this one, rather than a confident, hollow, neoclassical reference to "ill-fated Medea" of a "greater age." Landor prefers to suggest the greatness of the climb, of age itself.

He conceives his incident with the maximum of feeling —
to excess, even. I think that the poem is unhappily marred by
the lines succeeding the passage above, an attempt to inject
"the pathetic" and so prepare for the line, "He was more
changed than they were." Landor's willingness to push each
situation for emotion to its extreme and beyond is in this case
an irritation:

> *They lie three paces from him: such they lie*
> *As when he left them sleeping side by side,*
> *A mother's arm round each, a mother's cheeks*
> *Between them, flushed with happiness and love.*
> *He was more changed than they were, doomed. . . .*
> *lines 28–32*

Nevertheless, the poem's real power survives this mawkish instant, perhaps because the fault is so closely interrelated with
the source of power here and in "Sophocles to Poseidon": containment of savage, disproportionate emotion by the censoring,
modifying presence of the immutable heights. The disdain of
antiquity becomes part of Landor's political disdain. And the
political feeling, along with the other dimensions of the poem,
remains real in 1968.

Conclusion

I will close this study of Landor's poems by trying to let Landor
speak, as far as possible, in summary of his own career. The
poem which most nearly speaks in that way is the "Apology for
Gebir." Written in fact more than half a century after *Gebir*, it
brings together in a lighter tone many aspects of the themes
I have discussed. That is, the devotion to antiquity is defended
with a surface gentleness, within the context of leveling, dis-
passionate time. The time is historical, but also personal: that
an old man is defending the work of his youth is important, in
all of its comic implications, as is demonstrated with the opening words — word, one could say:

> *Sixty the years since* Fidler *bore*
> *My grouse bag up the Bala moor,* . . .

The clearly recollected expedition on horseback in Wales strikes another characteristic note; the poet's affection for the welcome remoteness of nature. "Nature" meaning not, as Robert Frost's professor maintained,[31] "scenery," but rather (as I believe Frost to have meant) man's life *in* scenery — all of one's general concerns outside of art. For Landor to have said that he loved this "nature" above art was, for him, strong and rather daring language. Both nature and art are worthy of love because they are remote from the lamentably unavoidable pettiness of immediate existence. The "Apology," in fact, is a defense of concerns, in life and literature, which might be called "remote." He defends the uses of the remote.

The self-mocking gentleness of tone of course contains a hard vein of irony. Landor here addresses the world, telling it once again how aloof he is, and for once makes that profession without fury in his voice — but there is something like fury waiting in nearly every tight tetrameter line. Barely restrained until the final haughty blast is the weary rage which probably found its most compact expression in a line from "Farewell to Italy":

> *I did believe (what have I not believed?)*

The attitude compressed in those eight words is Disillusion — Romanticism's answer to the preceding age's *nil admirari*. In-

---

31. In the following poem:

> *Lucretius* versus *the Lake Poets*
> "Nature I Loved; and next to Nature, Art."
> *Dean, adult education may seem silly.*
> *What of it though? I got some willy-nilly*
> *The other evening at your college deanery.*
> *And grateful for it (Let's not be facetious!)*
> *For I thought Epicurus and Lucretius*
> *By Nature meant the Whole Goddam Machinery.*
> *But you say that in college nomenclature*
> *The only meaning possible for Nature*
> *In Landor's quatrain would be Pretty Scenery.*
> *Which makes opposing it to Art absurd*
> *I grant you — if you're sure about the word.*
> *God bless the Dean and make his deanship plenary.*

deed, the phrase constitutes a fine definition by example of "Romanticism" in one of its kinds — and yet retains a slight shade of Augustan detachment.

Throughout the "Apology" disillusion finds its way half-way back to the eighteenth century, through the wit of philosophic unconcern. Much of the poem's delight is in the controlled combinations of tone. That initial, offhand "Sixty" has about it the quality of revery, but also suggests a perspective which scoffs at the fussy, passing quarrels of literary taste: time is long, and even this venerable life is short.

A similar combination of tones inheres in Landor's simultaneous defense of the classic and the out-of-the-way. The borders between "Romantic" and "Classical" have blurred considerably in the century of Landor's life; he defends himself against an orthodoxy of attention to the present and immediate and bases his defense upon the remote, Romantic qualities of the classical past. Thus, a great many overtones of context as well as form pervade his restatement of a hoary truism:

> *Manners have changed; but hearts are yet*
> *The same, and will be while they beat.*

Even without its context, the couplet precisely defines its distance from its many forebears in Pope. The emotion on the enjambed "yet" marks the difference; remove the runover —

> *Manners have changed; but hearts are yet the same,*
> *And will be while they beat. . . .*

— and one has four-fifths of a closed couplet, with appropriate caesura and consequent change in tone.

Reminiscent of the portraits in Augustan satire, Landor's Dapper embodies an unsympathetic critical orthodoxy. He utters nearly one quarter of the poem's lines and defines the grounds for the argument: is Landor's pride really snobbery, and is his detachment really a retreat? And if hearts *are* yet the same, why seek such quaint, remote ones?

> *Dapper, who may perhaps have seen*
> *My name in some late magazine,*
> *Among a dozen or a score*

Which interest wise people more,
Wonders if I can be the same
To whom poor Southey augured fame,
Erring, as usual, in his choice
Of one who mocks the public voice,
And fancies two or three are worth
Far more than all the rest on earth. . . .
"Landor should have done better far
Had he observed the northern star;
Or Bloomfield might have shown the way
To one who always goes astray;
He might have tried his pen upon
The living, not the dead and gone.
Are turban'd youths and muffled belles
Extinct among the Dardanelles?
Is there no scimitar, . . .

Dapper is referring to the glories of the Crimean war, and wonders why Landor must turn to the obscure past if he is writing a poem about the East. Dapper mentions several of the British leaders in the Crimean, including the infamous Cardigan of the Light Brigade.

Much of Landor's response is, naturally, implicit in Dapper's speech. The Crimean was not an attractive campaign; but to say this is to play into Dapper's hands, it may seem. Is Landor confessing that the past is prettier, or easy to make pretty? Part of the answer is quantitative, already implied by the "Two or three" [32] as opposed to the "dozen or a score." Because the past is large and manifold, the present small and single, the past offers a wider selection as well as an easier one. Very few true poets — or true heroes — are alive at one time. Furthermore, those few are not always easy to distinguish, as Dapper's critique of Southey, and his own reference to Bloomfield,[33] suggest. The argument is classic.

32. Landor, whose taste appears to have rarefied with passing time, changed the line from its original version, which was "ten or twelve." I don't feel that this weakens my argument.

33. Robert Bloomfield (1766–1823) was a poet, shoemaker, and expert on the making of Aeolian harps. His *The Farmer's Boy* sold 26,000 copies and was praised somewhat by Hazlitt.

A less likely referent is Nathaniel Bloomfield, a tailor. His *An Essay on*

But Landor's full defense is contained in the passages which precede and follow Dapper's remarks. The first of these is reticent and oblique, the second quite the opposite. The poem's structure resembles what might happen if Landor struck one tone and then was irritated by Dapper.

The opening passage takes a tone far from the Augustan. The detachment of this voice more resembles that of the nineteenth-century amateur. The kindly old gentleman loves horses, moors, and mountains — more, perhaps, than letters. For the first twelve lines or so, the statement appears to be a mild admonition that poetry, after all, is not everything. And this tone is echoed by the regret, while praising Southey, that poets do not have the virtues — and good manners — which they might. Even considered in such terms the passage is charming:

> *Sixty the years since* Fidler *bore*
> *My grouse bag up the Bala moor,*
> *Above the lake, along the lea*
> *Where gleams the darkly yellow Dee.*
> *Thro' crags, o'er cliffs, I carried there*
> *My verses with paternal care,*
> *But left them, and went home again*
> *To wing the birds upon the plain.*
> *With heavier luggage half-forgot,*
> *For many months they followed not.*
> *When over Tawey's sands they came,*
> *Brighter flew up my winter flame,*
> *And each old cricket sang alert*
> *With joy that they had come unhurt.*
> *Gebir! men shook their heads in doubt*
> *If we were sane: few made us out,*
> *Beside one stranger; in his heart*
> *We after held no niggard part.*
> *The songs of every age he knew,*
> *But only sang the pure and true.*
> *Poet he was, yet was his smile*
> *Without a tinge of gall or guile.*
> *Such lived, 'tis said, in ages past;*
> *Who knows if Southey was the last?*
> *Dapper, who may perhaps. . . .*

War, in Blank Verse was published in 1803, the same year as the revised *Gebir.*

As the Welch place names suggest, the incident is true. It is also true that Southey discovered *Gebir* long before he met Landor, wrote an extremely admiring review, and started the poem's high underground reputation with Coleridge and others. (De Quincey and Shelley were other centers of the reputation.) The facts of the poem are actual facts of Landor's career. He speaks not as Sophocles or Aspasia, but as Landor.

Nevertheless, I believe that the passage is allegorical. Landor's frequent metaphorical use of heights and plains, and his firm disapproval of shooting,[34] support the belief. The shooting is there because it suits the tone and the meaning. The time from the grouse season to the winter of sixty years ago represents the time from sixty years ago to the present. *Gebir* is a long poem in blank verse, a kind of poem which Landor (unlike Southey and many others) abandoned early in his career. "The plain," then, is a kind of poetry removed from the epic further than *Gebir* (which, Landor decided years after composition, was not really an epic). But as the crickets and the winter flame affirm, the half-forgotten poem, recalled and defended so much later, is definitely not disavowed.

And sneaking into the mild introductory passage, Landor's haughty theme emerges: Southey praised the true, few praised or even understood *Gebir*, Southey praised *Gebir*; *ergo*, only few write true poems, and few can discern them when they first appear. Landor's theme is selection — selection, and moderation, which is the tonal effect of the passage. The position taken against Dapper is in this measure Johnsonian: the past is more refined than the present because it has been subject to more scrutiny and selection. What is remote is often the more visible to those who see well, and the distance which Landor's poem traveled before it came again to his attention qualifies his enthusiasm as authentic. The Landorian motif of distance thus emerges in an optimistic and rationalistic light; the eighteenth-century element in the poem's rhetorical flavor accords perfectly with its theme.

34. See Super, *Walter Savage Landor*, pp. 533, 580.

Certainly, this material is muted and implicit in the opening passage, and the variation from the bland tone at "in doubt/If we were sane" is apparently self-mocking. Dapper has not yet had his say. When he has, he concludes his speech with a question:

> *"Do heroes of old times surpass*
> *Cardigan, Somerset, Dundas?*
> *Do the Sigaean mounds inclose*
> *More corses than Death swept from those?"*

Landor, begging permission to respond with a question, begins in the spirit of moderation which provides support and balance for the spirit of selectivity which he is really putting forward more urgently.

He soon sweeps on, however, toward a profession of commitment. The developing change of tone toward ferocious, open statement emerges as Landor's first sentence carries across four lines. (The handling of the measure, as the reference to "Hudibras" indicates, has been meticulously conscious; Dapper speaks entirely in closed couplets, but Landor does not):

> *No, no: but let me ask in turn*
> *Whether, whene'er Corinthian urn,*
> *With Ivied faun upon the rim*
> *Invites, I may not gaze on him?*

This genteel plea for differences of taste develops into a plea on behalf of the taste which is always the same, correct taste. The many kinds of beauty emphasize that authentic beauty is a rare thing, found by considering a very wide range of sources. And remote or ancient subjects are defended as hard, as demanding energy; because they require more human resource, they are more human and less pedantic. Milton and Butler are both beautiful. And a more recent, very pedantic poet exemplifies the supposedly "immediate"; Young advanced the "dramatic lyric," the meditation *en scene*, and Landor condemns the resultant emphasis on mood and atmosphere. Soft, less vigorous, such introspection leads to mere verbal effects because it is sedentary, static, self-contained:

gaze on him?
I love all beauty: I can go
At times from Gainsboro' to Watteau;
Even after Milton's thorough-bass
I bear the rhymes of Hudibras,
And find more solid wisdom there
Than pads professor's easy chair:
But never sit I quiet long
Where broidered cassock floats round Young;
Whose pungent essences perfume
And quirk and quibble trim the tomb;
Who thinks the holy bread too plain,
And in the chalice pours champagne.

After "Watteau" above, the poem as first published contained the couplet, "Never from Titian's Alpine scene/To Morland's style, however clean." Morland, painter of extremely popular rustic scenes, served a purpose similar to that of Bloomfield. Culling good art from ephemera is associated with the pursuit of subject; both processes require a good deal of care, tolerance, and discernment, as well as an awareness of how rare is the real thing. No subject is necessarily better than another, but antiquity offers firm ground, although demanding much energy. To seek far, in both pursuits, is to show strength, not to retreat.

Other ideas are combined in a characteristic way in the final lines. Landor's defense of Gebir's exotic fable is conducted partly on the neoclassical grounds that all times and places are essentially the same. At the same time, he puts a value on the remote and the ancient for the courage to venture which they inspire. Learning, to master what is difficult even to reach, is a Romantic adventure:

pours champagne.
I love old places and their climes,
By your acacia's crooked thorn,
Nor quit the syrinx for the chimes.
Manners have changed; but hearts are yet
The same, and will be while they beat.
Ye blame not those who wander o'er
Our earth's remotest wildest shore,
Nor scoff at seeking what is hid

> *Within one-chambered pyramid;*
> *Let me then, with my coat untorn*
> *Follow from Gades to the coast*
> *Of Egypt men thro' ages lost.*
> *Firm was my step on rocky steeps;*
> *Others slid down loose sandhill heaps.*
> *I knew where hidden fountains lay;*
> *Hoarse was their thirsty camels' bray;*
> *And presently fresh droves had past*
> *The beasts expiring on the waste.*

He is as lonely as Childe Harold, this classicist. The concluding image is a final proud assertion of the idea that time is a selector. The hidden fountains are not obscure or out of the way; they are hard to reach. They are the reward and the power for dealing with what is rocky and austere.

The finally-emerged Landorian arrogance is perhaps tempered somewhat by the image of the passing, fresh droves: who knows how many may pass one by, or how far. Time is long, history is more crowded every day, and eventually all, excepting perhaps the very, very great, must become "men thro' ages lost." Landor's repute, about which he pretended to care little, has been the subject for much scolding and worrying by his admirers. Yet it is natural that his fame be somewhat remote. Of course I think that he is to be read; I would not make an exclusive club of his poems. But their uncompromising voice comes largely from the personal core which is defined in the "Apology," a Mauberley-like voice which tempers self-pity with imperturbable confidence, stoicism with stinging rage. The poems which this personality produced should be cherished for their unique forging together of learning with Romantic sensibility, of passion with great conscious art.

Index